"Bob Thompson has captured the essence of morning and evening devotions and focuses on many salient subjects rarely considered by others. He has challenged me to a closer look."

—Paul L. Brown, BA, ThM, DMin,
Former Senior Pastor, First Baptist Church, Woodbridge VA
Former Senior Pastor, Abundant Life Baptist Church, Dumfries VA

"Any reader will discover a wealth of great insight into God's Word as you walk through this little book morning and evening. It will grab your heart and promote love and obedience in your life for our amazing Lord!"

—Steve Hammack
Senior Pastor, Anchor Church, Loganville GA

"I highly encourage this book to anyone desiring to take a closer daily walk with Jesus. Just as the physical body needs daily bread, so do our spiritual lives. This book sets the table for a meal with God in the morning and the evening. These devotionals will draw you personally into feasting on the Word and to drinking in His goodness through prayer. Each day is a reflection and a connection with the living God and the whole counsel of the Word."

—Todd Gaston
Senior Pastor, Mount Ararat Baptist Church, Stafford VA

Resources by Robert L. Thompson

G.R.A.C.E. Evangelism; Five Steps to Fulfilling God's Purpose in Sharing the Gospel. Xulon Press, 2011

A Closer Look

An Inspirational Collection of
Morning and Evening Devotionals

Robert L. Thompson

WESTBOW°
PRESS
A DIVISION OF THOMAS NELSON
& ZONDERVAN

Scripture references are from the King James Version (KJV) of the Holy Bible.

WestBow Press books may be ordered through booksellers or by contacting:

WestBow Press
A Division of Thomas Nelson & Zondervan
1663 Liberty Drive
Bloomington, IN 47403
www.westbowpress.com
1 (866) 928-1240

ISBN: 978-1-5127-0918-6 (sc)
ISBN: 978-1-5127-0919-3 (hc)
ISBN: 978-1-5127-0920-9 (e)

Library of Congress Control Number: 2015913274

Print information available on the last page.

WestBow Press rev. date: 08/14/2015

For Melissa

Preface

This series of daily devotionals is not intended to replace your daily reading of God's Word—the Holy Bible. Neither are they intended to replace the time you spend in prayer on a daily basis before the Lord Jesus Christ.

Instead, these devotionals are intended to encourage you to take a closer look at His Word each and every day.

These devotionals should be read over the course of a month and then repeated in subsequent months. When you begin using this book, it is not necessary to wait for the first day of the month; simply begin with the devotional for that day.

As you devote yourself to a daily quiet time of prayer and Bible study, may "The Lord bless thee, and keep thee: The Lord make his face shine upon thee, and be gracious unto thee: The Lord lift up his countenance upon thee, and give thee peace." (Numbers 6:24–26).

Robert L. Thompson
January 2014

Contents

The First Commandment

Thou shalt have no other gods before me.
—Exodus 20:3

The first commandment is not only the first in sequence but also the first in priority. It declares the authority of God, the author of the law, and it forms the foundation for the commandments that follow.

The children of Israel knew that these commandments were not merely solemn warnings developed by Moses on some mountaintop. "And God spake all these words, saying…" (Exodus 20:1). The children of Israel had been under the constant influence of idolatry and polytheism during four hundred years of captivity in Egypt. They were influenced by pagan worship once again when they finally arrived in the Promised Land of Canaan. God used their time during the wilderness journey to provide His law and set moral standards for the lives of the children of Israel. The Commandments are as important for us today as they were for the children of Israel more than two thousand years ago. God knows us too well to let us drift through life without the truth and surety of His loving guidance. "No other gods" means exactly that. God is to be number one in our lives. Jesus said, "Thou shalt worship the Lord thy God and him only shalt thou serve" (Luke 4:8). Nothing in your life—work, pleasure, sports, school, or friends—should come before Him. With such busy daily schedules, keeping God first can be difficult.

God desires us to experience communion with Him. He wants us to love Him, pray to Him, *listen* to Him, and read His Word daily. God wants us to be so focused on Him that we think about what would please Him before we make decisions, before we speak, and even before we engage in service for Him. He wants to maintain this close and personal relationship with us. This will only be realized if we make Him our number one priority.

Lord, help us to keep You first in everything we do.

Why Three Crosses?

Where they crucified him, and two other with him, on
either side one, and Jesus in the midst.

—John 19:18

I have often heard others wonder why there were only two thieves.
Why not three, four, or even more? I have also heard others ask
why Jesus was placed in the middle rather than on one side or the
other. "And with him they crucify two thieves; the one on his right
hand, and the other on his left" (Mark 15:27). For Christians, Jesus
is the centerpiece of our faith. Let us note the nature of thieves. A
thief is one who is guilty of larceny, which is the taking of personal
property without consent and with the intention of permanently
depriving the owner. As God's creation, we belong to Him. In a
sense, we act as thieves when we ignore God, depriving him of
what rightly belongs to Him – our commitment to Him.

But why were there only two thieves? Perhaps it was symbolic.
The Scriptures teach that there are only two ways to respond to
Jesus Christ: we will either accept Him or reject Him. Just as at
Calvary, some will reject Jesus to the very end of life. "And one of
the malefactors which were hanged railed on him, saying, if thou
be Christ, save thyself and us" (Luke 23:39). The very presence
of God did not affect the thief who rejected Him. Those who
accept Jesus will receive the gift of eternal life. We all deserve to
receive sin's penalty of death. "But the other answering rebuked
him, saying, Dost not thou fear God, seeing thou art in the same
condemnation? And we indeed justly; for we receive the due
reward of our deeds: but this man hath done nothing amiss. And
he said unto Jesus, Lord, remember me when thou comest into
thy kingdom" (vv. 40–42). Jesus willingly gave His life for all of
humankind. He will forgive the sins and grant the gift of eternal
life to those who believe and accept this truth. "And Jesus said
unto him, Verily I say unto thee, To day shalt thou be with me in
paradise" (v. 43).

Lord, help us to share this truth of eternal life.

The Second Commandment

Thou shalt not make unto thee any graven image.
—Exodus 20:4

Only God, the Creator of the universe, is worthy of praise and worship. Offer all praise and glory to Him, forever and ever.

While idolatry in the first commandment was spiritual, idolatry in the second commandment is physical. How foolish of humanity to think that a golden calf could replace God's omnipotence, omniscience, or omnipresence. Worshipping man-made objects and images is an insult to the love, honor, majesty, wisdom, holiness, mercy, and glory of God.

However, this commandment does not prohibit the artistic creation of heavenly objects and images that we may place around our homes and offices. In fact, angels were fashioned for the ark of the covenant. "And he made two cherubims of gold, beaten out of one piece made he them, on the two ends of the mercy seat" (Exodus 37:7). The second commandment does, however, prohibit any form of worship of these man-made objects and images. "Thou shalt not bow down thyself to them, nor serve them" (Exodus 20:5). Having objects and images of angels around your home is not idolatry. We become idolaters when these heavenly type objects and images become the focus of our worship. "I am the first, and I am the last; and beside me there is no God" (Isaiah 44:6).

Perhaps one of the best passages in Scripture for summarizing this calamity of humanity can be found in the Psalms. "The idols of the heathen are silver and gold, the work of men's hands. They have mouths, but they speak not; eyes have they, but they see not; they have ears, but they hear not; neither is there any breath in their mouths. They that make them are like unto them: so is every one that trusteth in them" (Psalm 135:15–18).

Lord, help us to worship only You, our Creator.

An Appropriate Position for Coming Home

And he arose, and came to his father, But when
he was yet a great way off, his father saw him, and
had compassion, and ran, and fell on his neck, and
kissed him.

—Luke 15:20

While this is commonly referred to as the parable of the prodigal
son, the central figure is the father. Note that every parable in Luke
15 deals with lost items. It is not coincidental that Christ directs
this parable to our attention about humanity's relationship to God.
While this passage could be viewed as one of redemption, a closer
look helps us to understand God's plan for revival and restoration
in the lives of His children.

First, consider the father. We clearly see relationship. While
the father knew what was best for his child, he allowed him to
choose the lifestyle he desired to live. Because of the father's love
for his child, he patiently awaited his son's return. The father
had compassion for his son. This is the type of love that Christ
explained and the father demonstrated. Second, consider the son. I
see relationship, rebellion, realization, and reaction in the son's life.
The son had relationship by birth. He demonstrated rebellion by
demanding what he thought would bring him happiness. Then he
realized that the world is not so kind to those who have exhausted
their material wealth, and his reaction to this realization was
accepting responsibility for his actions and returning home. The
son's most important reaction was returning home with humility.
However, the one "R" that is missing is restoration. We know from
the remainder of the parable that the father welcomed the son
home with open arms.

Finally, consider the appropriate position for coming home. The
father ran to his son and fell on his neck and kissed him. In order
for the father to "fall" on the son's neck, the son had to be kneeling
with his head bowed before his father.

Lord, help us to always show an attitude of humility.

Notes

The Third Commandment

Thou shalt not take the name of the LORD thy God
in vain.

—Exodus 20:7

In biblical times a person's name represented the essence of his
being—his nature, his personality, and even his character. In
many respects this still holds true today. "A good name is rather
to be chosen than great riches" (Proverbs 22:1). Many think that
merely restricting the use of God's name in profanity satisfies this
commandment. Limiting such sacrilegious speech is a worthy goal,
but it falls way short of the fulfillment of this commandment.

There are many names found in the Bible for God; the following
are but a few: El Shaddai (Lord God Almighty); El Elyon (The
Most High God); Adonai (Lord, Master); Yahweh (LORD, Jehovah);
Jehovah Rapha (The Lord Who Heals); Jehovah Tsidkenu (The
Lord Our Righteousness); Elohim (God); Jehovah (The Lord Will
Provide); Jehovah Shalom (The Lord Is Peace).

Spelling "LORD" with all capital letters, as in Exodus 20:7,
represents Yahweh. Yahweh represents the covenant relationship
God had with His people, the Israelites. This commandment is
directed to those who understand that God is holy and righteous,
because of their relationship with Him.

So what does it really mean to take the Lord's name "in vain"? "In
vain" can be interpreted as without effect, with no purpose, and
even in an improper or irreverent manner. It means that if we use
or associate God's name with anything that is not righteous and
holy, we have used God's name in vain. This includes times when
in the heat of the moment we flippantly say things like, "Jesus
Christ" and "OMG."

Lord, help us to never take Your name in vain.

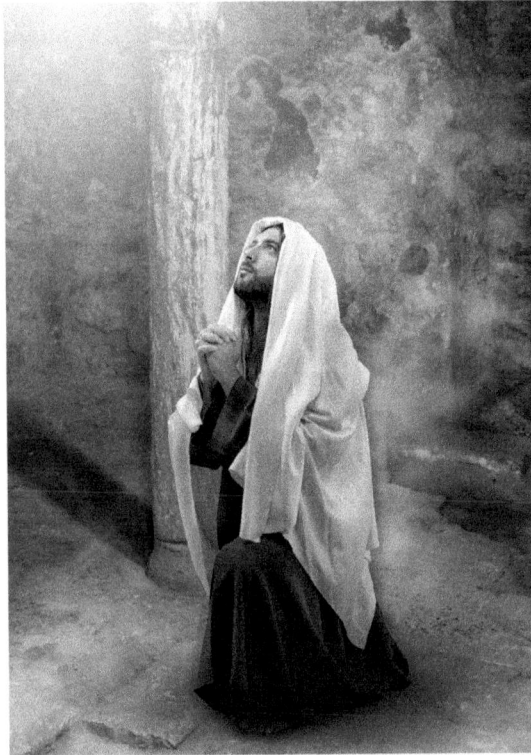

Going Farther with the Father

And he went a little farther, and fell on his face, and
prayed.

—Matthew 26:39

There are basically two ways to go farther with the Father: prayer
time and Bible study. No doubt, prayer in the life of a Christian is
not optional obedience—it is a discipline. Jesus clearly emphasized
"when" and not "if" by saying, "And when thou prayest" (Matthew
6:5). God's desire is that we have a devoted prayer life. "Continue
in prayer" (Colossians 4:2). We should envy Jesus' prayer life. "he
went out into a mountain to pray, and continued all night in prayer
to God" (Luke 6:12).

Bible study is also not optional obedience. It is a discipline. The
best discipline for Bible study is reading God's Word. "Study to
shew thyself approved unto God, a workman that needeth not to
be ashamed, rightly dividing the word of truth" (2 Timothy 2:15).
How often should we pray and read God's Word? How often do we
face problems, temptation, and pressure? We should pray and read
the Bible every day. The following are examples of going farther
with the Father.

Obedience: "And hereby we do know that we know him, if we keep
his Commandments. He that saith, I know him, and keepeth not
his commandments, is a liar, and the truth is not in him" (1 John
2:3–4). Only a close relationship with the Father will permit us to
regularly demonstrate obedience to Him.

Behavior: "He that saith he abideth in him ought himself also so to
walk, even as he walked" (v. 6). Only a close relationship with the
Father will permit us to live a lifestyle that honors Christ.

Love: "He that loveth his brother abideth in the light, and there
is none occasion of stumbling in him" (v. 10). Only a close
relationship with the Father will permit us to love like this.

Lord, help us to go farther with You.

11

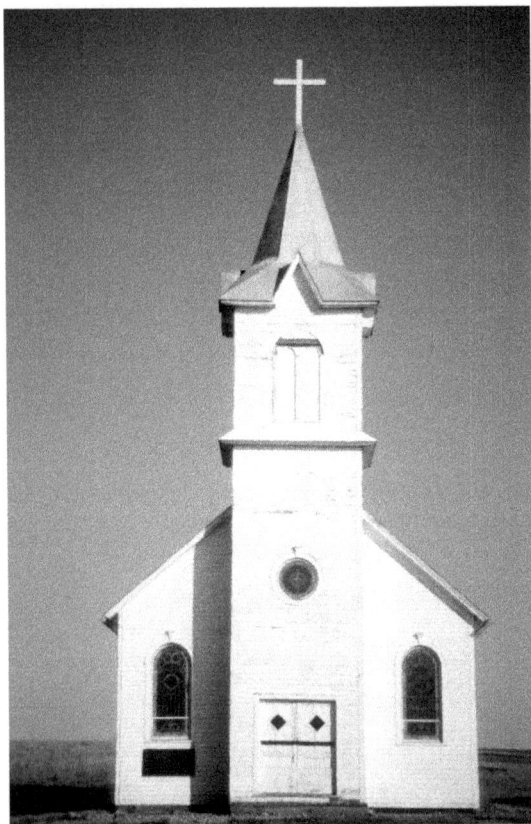

The Fourth Commandment

Remember the Sabbath Day, to keep it holy.
　　　　　　　　　　　　　—Exodus 20:8

This Sabbath (seventh) day was made holy by God and set aside as a day of rest. The Sabbath is remembered from the creation events in Genesis 2. "And on the seventh day God ended his work which he had made…And God blessed the seventh day, and sanctified it: because that in it he had rested from all his work which God created and made" (Genesis 2:2–3).

While the Sabbath day is intended to be a day of rest, it is more than that. The Sabbath was also to be a sign and a covenant for all generations between God and His people. "My sabbaths ye shall keep: for it is a sign between me and you … that ye may know that I am the LORD that doth sanctify you" (Exodus 31:13). "The children of Israel shall keep the sabbath, to observe the sabbath throughout their generations, for a perpetual covenant. It is a sign … for ever: for in six days the LORD made heaven and earth, and on the seventh day he rested, and was refreshed" (vv. 16–17). It was intended to be a sign, as the rainbow was God's promise never to flood the earth again. Our Sabbath day should be used as a day of rest and commitment. We should focus on God Himself, His lordship, and most importantly, His love for mankind.

> If thou turn away thy foot … from doing thy
> pleasure on my holy day; and call the sabbath a
> delight, the holy of the LORD, honourable; and
> shalt honour him, not doing thine own ways, nor
> finding thine own pleasure … : Then shalt thou
> delight thyself in the LORD; and I will cause thee
> to ride upon the high places of the earth … for the
> mouth of the LORD hath spoken it.
> —Isaiah 58:13–14

Lord, help us to keep the Sabbath day holy.

13

Notes

Faith—More Than Hope

Now faith is the substance of things hoped for.
—Hebrews 11:1

Faith is the substance; not faith is hope. Faith has been defined as a belief not based on logical proof or material evidence. The Bible tells us what our substance is. Jesus said to Thomas, "Reach hither thy finger, and behold my hands; and reach hither thy hand, and thrust it into my side: and be not faithless, but believing" (John 20:27). Our substance is the living Christ.

What does the Bible have to say about the resurrection and faith? "If in this life only we have hope in Christ, we are of all men most miserable" (1 Corinthians 15:19). This is after Paul stated, "Now if Christ be preached that he rose from the dead, how say some among you that there is no resurrection of the dead? But if there be no resurrection … then is Christ not risen: and if Christ be not risen, then is our preaching vain, and your faith is also vain" (1 Corinthians 15:12–14). Our faith is in the risen Christ.

Other passages proclaim the resurrection of Christ. "He is not here: for he is risen, as he said" (Matthew 28:6). "And he saith unto them, Be not affrighted: Ye seek Jesus … which was crucified: he is risen; he is not here" (Mark 16:6). Jesus proclaimed this truth to Martha: "I am the resurrection and the life" (John 11:25).

The certainty of going to heaven is more than hope. "These things have I written unto you that believe on the name of the Son of God; that ye may know that ye have eternal life" (1 John 5:13). You can know for certain that you have eternal life. "But now is Christ risen from the dead … For as in Adam all die, even so in Christ shall all be made alive" (1 Corinthians 15:20, 22). Our faith is substance— the living Christ. Have faith and express your faith in Jesus Christ today.

Lord, help us to live a faith that is more than hope.

Notes

The Fifth Commandment

> Honour thy father and thy mother.
>
> —Exodus 20:12

We now come to the first commandment that deals with man's relationship to man. The first four commandments dealt with man's relationship to God. It is interesting that God chose to have the fifth commandment identify the importance of each person's relationship to their parents. The Bible teaches that this is the first commandment with promise to ensure "that thy days may be long upon the land which the LORD thy God giveth thee" (Exodus 20:12).

Many parents use this commandment to teach their children about how to behave toward their parents. While this is certainly good counsel, this commandment is directed toward adults as much as it is to the younger generation. The truth of this commandment rests in the fact that regardless of age, we are to honor our fathers and mothers.

How do we do that? Our fathers and mothers are the most important people in our lives and as such, they should provide the most importance influence. With this in mind, we are to treat them with respect and dignity continually throughout our lifetimes.

One of the best and easiest practical ways to honor our fathers and mothers is to verbally express this respect whenever the appropriate opportunity arises, and to let them know that we love them. My parents use to say that "actions speak louder than words," which leads to the next best way to honor our fathers and mothers. We must regularly demonstrate honor for our parents by living in such a way that honors them. Visiting and calling our parents regularly demonstrates that they are important. We should also actively seek opportunities to do things for them—most of all, when they least expect it.

Lord, help us to honor our fathers and our mothers.

17

Notes

Talitha Cumi

Talitha cumi; which is, being interpreted, Damsel, I say
unto thee, arise.

—Mark 5:41

By the very word of God, miracles happen—and they still happen
today. Did Christ need to take the damsel by the hand? We know
from other examples in Scripture that Christ merely had to say
the word and people were healed. In one example a centurion
beseeched Jesus to heal his servant who was in his home. "Jesus
saith unto him, I will come and heal him" (Matthew 8:7). This
centurion expressed to Jesus that if He would but speak the word,
his servant would be healed. Jesus marveled at this response
and stated that He had not found so great a faith anywhere in
Israel. When another man, Jairus, asked for help, why did Jesus
accompany him to his home? He went because he was asked to
go. "I pray thee, come and lay thy hands on her, that she may be
healed; and she shall live" (Mark 5:23). Jesus went with him. There
was another reason Jesus went with Jairus. The key to this reason is
found in several verses: *Be not afraid, only believe.* And he suffered
no man to follow him, save Peter, and James, and John" (vv. 36–
37). "And he charged them straitly that no man should know it" (v.
43). It was lesson time.

Jesus wanted to demonstrate the power of God. God will
demonstrate His power to those willing to be obedient and follow
Him. Some want to hear and see the power of God, and some
refuse to acknowledge God. Note that Jesus took His inner circle
with Him (Peter, James, and John). Jesus commanded that no man
should know it, because of those standing outside of the damsel's
door who laughed at him in scorn. Their unbelief caused them
to miss out on witnessing God's power and glory. May we be like
the centurion and Jairus. They both asked for something from the
Lord, in faith. "But let him ask in faith, nothing wavering" (James
1:6). Ask today—in faith.

Lord, help us to ask in faith, nothing wavering.

Notes

The Sixth Commandment

Thou shalt not kill.

—Exodus 20:13

The New International Version (NIV) translation of the Hebrew word *rasah* in this passage is actually "murder." The difference between "murder" and "kill" is that "murder" involves premeditation. Premeditation was implied in the following passage from Genesis: "Whoso sheddeth man's blood, by man shall his blood be shed" (Genesis 9:6). The "shedding of blood" is synonymous with "murder," carrying with it the malicious willful intent to take the life of another human being.

A question that often arises with the discussion of this commandment is the topic of war. Throughout history, war has plagued humanity. Man's fallen nature and sin have caused this evil that we know as war. That being said, every man has a right to defend himself, his family, his homeland, and yes, even his allies during times of violent aggression. In the context of war, there is a difference between killing and unjust killing (murder). During my service in the U.S. military, I was able to further reconcile my Christian beliefs with this commandment and a "just war." "Just war" has been defined as a war that is deemed to be morally and/or theologically justifiable.

Every human being has value in the sight of God. No man has the right to take the life of another human being. Unfortunately, our nation is plagued today with many types of murder. These include homicides, suicides, and abortion. These evils directly violate "Thou shalt not murder." The good news is that God has provided a remedy for this sin that plagues our nation.

"If my people, which are called by my name, shall humble themselves, and pray, and seek my face, and turn from their wicked ways; then will I hear from heaven, and will forgive their sin, and will heal their land" (2 Chronicles 7:14).

Lord, please guide us as a nation.

Notes

God Is Faithful

God is faithful.

—1 Corinthians 10:13

God in Christ provided many of life's examples for our lives. He taught us obedience, how to pray, and how to love. And He taught us about faith. "Without faith, it is impossible to please him" (Hebrews 11:6). Being faithful is essential to our relationship with Jesus Christ. After all, what better example of faithfulness can God provide us than the example of His faithfulness to us during our temptations?

We will never experience a temptation that God has not seen before. God knows all of our situations. He knows every temptation we have faced and every one that we will ever face. We know that temptations do not come from God. "Let no man say when he is tempted, I am tempted of God: for God cannot be tempted with evil, neither tempteth he any man" (James 1:13). Our temptations come from evil. What is the difference between a test and a temptation? Temptations come with enticements. "But every man is tempted, when he is drawn away of his own lust, and enticed" (v. 14). Evil will always prompt (entice) us to do evil.

"But God is faithful, who will not suffer you to be tempted above that ye are able" (1 Corinthians 10:13) If anyone is going to be on my side, I want it to be God. It is comforting to know that God knows we have temptations. It is also comforting to know that He controls the level at which evil tempts us.

God knows exactly where we are in our spiritual walk. He knows where I am strong and where I am weak. He will not allow me to be tempted above that which I am able, "but will with the temptation also make a way to escape, that ye may be able to bear it" (v. 13). While God allows us to be tempted, He promises that we will be able to bear the burden through His power.

Lord, thank You for being faithful; help us to be faithful.

Notes

The Seventh Commandment

Thou shalt not commit adultery.

—Exodus 20:14

Adultery involves a violation of the most intimate covenant act found within the bond of marriage. Violation of this covenant act damages the trust within the relationship between a married man and woman. This occurs when a married man or woman chooses to participate in this intimate act with someone other than his or her spouse.

It was God's intent that this intimate covenant act be reserved for the institution of marriage between one man and one woman, and it was clearly expressed in both Genesis and Ephesians. "Therefore shall a man leave his father and his mother, and shall cleave unto his wife: and they shall be one flesh" (Genesis 2:24). "For this cause shall a man leave his father and mother, and shall be joined unto his wife, and they two shall be one flesh" (Ephesians 5:31).

This oneness was not only intended to be physical, but also psychological, emotional, and spiritual. Jesus explained the spiritual nature and violation of this intimate covenant act in Matthew. "Ye have heard that it was said ..., Thou shalt not commit adultery: But I say unto you, That whosoever looketh on a woman to lust after her hath committed adultery with her already in his heart" (Matthew 5:27–28).

The marriage relationship between a man and a woman is symbolic of the relationship between God and man. They are both exclusive. It is a covenant relationship and an eternal relationship. God is a jealous God, thus demonstrating the tie between the seventh and the first commandments. "For I the Lord thy God am a jealous God" (Exodus 20:5). Anything in our lives that is more important than our relationship with God and His Son, Jesus Christ, could be considered as spiritual adultery.

Lord, help us not to commit adultery.

Notes

Thy Kingdom Come

Thy kingdom come.

—Matthew 6:10

The statement "Thy kingdom come" in Matthew 6 is often viewed as a prayer requesting Christ's return either for the rapture or for the second coming. The Lord's Prayer is actually a model prayer that provides us direction for our daily prayer and quiet time. What are the implications of this?

To truly understand this passage, we need to have an understanding of what "the kingdom" means. *The Baptist Faith and Message* provides the following definition: "The Kingdom of God includes both His general sovereignty over the universe and His particular kingship over men who willfully acknowledge Him as King."[1] In the context of this passage, the Lord's Prayer applies to God's particular kingship over men who willfully acknowledge Him as King. Matthew Henry commented, "Christ saw it needful to give a new directory for prayer, to show his disciples what must ordinarily be the *manner and method* of their prayer … we are here taught to pray that that kingdom might come which did come when the spirit was poured out."[2]

Jesus said the kingdom of God was at hand because of His presence. In the context of the Lord's Prayer, "Thy kingdom come" means kingdom presence or that we should pray for God to grant us His presence on a daily basis. God willingly does this by indwelling us with His Holy Spirit. "Jesus came into Galilee, preaching the gospel of the kingdom of God, And saying, The time is fulfilled, and the kingdom of God is at hand: repent ye, and believe the gospel" (Mark 1:14–15).

Every aspect of the Lord's Prayer should be prayed on a daily basis. How often should we pray for His kingdom presence and His will to be done? "Thy kingdom come, Thy will be done in earth, as it is in heaven." We should pray this prayer daily.

Lord, teach us to pray for Your kingdom presence daily.

27

Notes

The Eighth Commandment

Thou shalt not steal.

–Exodus 20:15

Stealing is to intentionally take someone's property without legal authority or without permission, with the intent of keeping that property and not returning it to the rightful owner. God's command against stealing is repeated in many Bible texts. A few include: "Neither shalt thou steal" (Deuteronomy 5:19). "Thou shalt not steal" (Romans 13:9). "Let him that stole steal no more" (Ephesians 4:28).

Stealing is an "umbrella" term commonly referred to in many cultures as theft, robbery, shoplifting, larceny, burglary, embezzling, and even plagiarizing. Every culture in the world today has severe penalties for the crime of stealing. After all, it was two thieves who were crucified with the Lord Jesus Christ.

Stealing violates the personal character trait of integrity. Integrity involves continually living a lifestyle of truthfulness and honesty. God's desire is that all men and women live a lifestyle of integrity. "And as for me, thou upholdest me in mine integrity" (Psalm 41:12). "The LORD shall judge the people: judge me, O LORD, according to my righteousness, and according to mine integrity that is in me" (Psalm 7:8).

Stealing is man's blatant disregard of God's promised provision. "According as his divine power hath given unto us all things that pertain unto life and godliness, through the knowledge of him that hath called us to glory and virtue" (2 Peter 1:3). "Give us this day our daily bread" (Matthew 6:11). "But my God shall supply all your need according to his riches in glory by Christ Jesus" (Philippians 4:19). Yes, beloved, the Lord will provide.

Lord, help us to understand that You will provide.

Notes

A.S.K.

Ask, and it shall be given you; seek, and ye shall find;
knock, and it shall be opened unto you.
—Matthew 7:7

I pray that the simplicity of this verse will not prohibit our exercise of this command. *Asking* should be prayer for what we know and understand to be God's will. "And this is the confidence that we have in him, that, if we ask anything according to his will, he heareth us" (1 John 5:14). An effective asking prayer life requires us to abide in Christ. "If ye abide in me, and my words abide in you, ye shall ask what ye will, and it shall be done unto you" (John 15:7). God grants His wisdom to all who ask. "If any of you lack wisdom, let him ask of God that giveth to all men liberally" (James 1:5). If we don't have, it is because we have not asked, expecting to receive. "Ye have not, because ye ask not" (4:2).

Seeking is prayer we voice when searching for God's will. We seek God through prayer and Bible study. Our priority should be seeking God first. "But seek ye first the kingdom of God and his righteousness" (Matthew 6:33). Christ demonstrated the importance of seeking God's will. "I seek not mine own will, but the will of the Father which hath sent me" (John 5:30). God has promised to reward those who faithfully seek him. "He is a rewarder of them that diligently seek him" (Hebrews 11:6).

Knocking is prayer for discovering the will of God. Before we knock, we need to make sure we have answered Christ's knocking. "Behold, I stand at the door, and knock: if any man hear my voice, and open the door, I will come in to him" (Revelation 3:20). "Yea, if thou criest after knowledge … Then shalt thou understand the fear of the Lord, and find the knowledge of God" (Proverbs 2:3, 5). "For every one that asketh receiveth; and he that seeketh findeth; and to him that knocketh it shall be opened" (Matthew 7:8).

Lord, help us to ask, seek, and knock.

Notes

The Ninth Commandment

Thou shalt not bear false witness against thy neighbor.
—Exodus 20:16

The Hebrew translation of this verse implies answering a matter falsely against your neighbor in a court of law. God established that a person could not be convicted in a court of law by the word of a single witness. "One witness shall not rise up against a man for any iniquity, or for any sin, in any sin that he sinneth: at the mouth of two witnesses, or at the mouth of three witnesses, shall the matter be established" (Deuteronomy 19:15).

Once a person swears an oath to tell the truth during an official judicial proceeding and then tells lies, it is perjury. This commandment goes further than merely the sin of perjury; it includes all forms of lying. "Ye shall not steal, neither deal falsely, neither lie one to another" (Leviticus 19:11).

If there is anything that I fear the most, it would be doing something that God hates. "These six things doth the Lord hate … a lying tongue … A false witness that speaketh lies" (Proverbs 6:16–19). In these four verses, God emphatically stated twice that He hates lying.

There are many other texts in Scripture that warn against lying. "Let the lying lips be put to silence" (Psalm 31:18). "The mouth of them that speak lies shall be stopped" (63:11). "Deliver my soul, O Lord, from lying lips" (120:2). "He that hideth hatred with lying lips, and he that uttereth a slander, is a fool" (Proverbs 10:18). "A false witness shall not be unpunished, and he that speaketh lies shall perish" (19:9). "But your iniquities have separated between you and your God, and your sins have hid his face from you, that he will not hear … your lips have spoken lies … they trust in vanity, and speak lies" (Isaiah 59:2–4).

Lord, help us not to lie.

Notes

God Provides, Man Denies

For all that is in the world, the lust of the flesh, and
the lust of the eyes, and the pride of life, is not of the
Father, but is of the world.

—1 John 2:16

Even in the Garden of Eden, man denied what God had provided.
Note how Eve failed in all three areas. "And when the woman saw
that the tree was good for food, and that it was pleasant to the eyes,
and a tree to be desired to make one wise, she took of the fruit
thereof, and did eat" (Genesis 3:6). "Good for food" fulfilled her
lust of the flesh; being "pleasant to the eyes" fulfilled her lust of the
eyes; and a tree to be "desired to make one wise" fulfilled her pride
of life.

God has warned us about the lust of the flesh: "Walk in the Spirit,
and ye shall not fulfill the lust of the flesh" (Galatians 5:16).
"Abstain from fleshly lusts, which war against the soul" (1 Peter
2:11). God has warned us about the lust of the eyes: "Having eyes
full of adultery, and that cannot cease from sin" (2 Peter 2:14). God
has warned us about the pride of life: "The wicked, through the
pride of his countenance, will not seek after God: God is not in all
his thoughts" (Psalm 10:4).

God also provided something else. "And out of the ground made
the LORD God to grow every tree that is pleasant to the sight,
and good for food; the tree of life also in the midst of the garden"
(Genesis 2:9). Fortunately, Adam and Eve did not eat from the Tree
of Life. "And the LORD God said, Behold, the man is become as
one of us, to know good and evil: and now, lest he put forth his
hand, and take also of the tree of life, and eat, and live for ever: …
So he drove out the man" (Genesis 3:22, 24). Sadly, man continues
to choose the lust of the flesh, the lust of the eyes, and the pride of
life that keep him from what God continues to provide: life. Gladly
accept God's provision today.

Lord, help us to receive and gladly accept Your provision.

Notes

The Tenth Commandment

Thou shalt not covet.

—Exodus 20:17

We covet when we earnestly desire to have those things belonging to others that we have no right to have. God tells us to be content with the things that we have. "Be content with such things as ye have: for he hath said, I will never leave thee, nor forsake thee" (Hebrews 13:5). If we are not satisfied with the things we have been provided by God's provision, we blatantly express dissatisfaction with those things He has provided.

This covetousness is idolatry. "Mortify therefore your members which are upon the earth … and covetousness, which is idolatry" (Colossians 3:5). James warns us about the evil temptations that cause us to covet because of our own desires and the unfortunate results. "Let no man say when he is tempted, I am tempted of God: for God cannot be tempted with evil, neither tempteth he any man: But every man is tempted, when he is drawn away of his own lust, and enticed. Then when lust hath conceived, it bringeth forth sin: and sin, when it is finished, bringeth forth death" (James 1:13–15).

Be not deceived; it is not God who tempts man. Unfortunately, the nature of success in America today feeds the fire of individual achievement. Greed, envy, and excessive desires have replaced moderation in our culture. Billboards, magazine advertisements, and television commercials all promote a self-aggrandizement mentality and attitude.

God gave us clear guidance that life is not about possessions. "Take heed, and beware of covetousness: for a man's life consisteth not in the abundance of the things which he possesseth" (Luke 12:15). A life that pleases God will not be spent going after the "next best thing."

Lord, help us not to covet.

37

Notes

The Church of the Laodiceans

And unto the angel of the church of the Laodiceans
write …

—Revelation 3:14

Here we have the last of the seven churches that Jesus addressed, and
unfortunately, He had nothing good to say about this church. If the
intent of the outline of the seven churches in Revelation serves as a
prophetical preview of the seven great periods of Christendom from
Pentecost to the rapture, then we can say that we are nearer to the
rapture today than ever before. Consider how God has been stripped
from our society. We have removed prayer, the Bible, and the Ten
Commandments from our schools. The true intent of "separation of
church and state" has been reinterpreted as "separation of church from
state." Immoral and unethical behavior is rampant in America today.

We see the church of the Laodiceans as the "lukewarm" or
"worldly" church. The name means "people's rights." The most
striking criticism Christ has for this church is contained in His
address to "the church *of* the Laodiceans." Every other church
referenced in Revelation 2 and 3 is identified by its location, not by
its ownership. Note: "*of* Ephesus," "*in* Smyrna," "*in* Pergamos," etc.
Not Laodicea. The Laodicean church did not belong to Christ; it
belonged to the Laodiceans.

The next most striking criticism Christ had was that their works
were "lukewarm." "I know thy works, that thou art neither cold
nor hot … because thou art lukewarm … I will spue thee out of my
mouth" (Revelation 3:15–16). The Laodiceans were familiar with
luke-warmness because they piped water in by aqueducts, making
their water lukewarm by the time that it reached them. "I will spue
thee out of my mouth." They knew exactly what that meant. You
might say "lukewarm" today, meaning "who cares." Who cares if I
don't pray regularly? Who cares if I don't study my Bible regularly?
Who cares? … Christ cares.

Lord, help us to stay faithful in all things.

Notes

A New Commandment

A new commandment I give unto you, that ye love one
another; as I have loved you.

—John 13:34

Is this a new commandment? This sounds like an old
commandment: "Thou shalt love thy neighbor as thyself"
(Leviticus 19:18). We have already been instructed to love each
other. "Jesus said unto him, Thou shalt love the Lord thy God with
all thy heart, and with all thy soul, and with all thy mind. This
is the first and great commandment. And the second is like unto
it, Thou shalt love thy neighbour as thyself" (Matthew 22:37–39).
The Lord couldn't have been any clearer. He commands us to love
others.

If we examine the context of this passage, we discover clues about
this new commandment. "Jesus knew his hour was come that he
should depart out of this world unto the Father, having loved his
own which were in the world, he loved them unto the end" (John
13:1). Jesus said, "Little children, yet a little while I am with you"
(John 13:33). Jesus knew He would be departing, that His presence
with man was about to change. Jesus then gave us this new
commandment that had to do with the new covenant: "Behold, the
days come, saith the LORD, that I will make a new covenant with
the house of Israel … I will put my law in their inward parts, and
write it in their hearts" (Jeremiah 31:31, 33).

This new commandment has to do with the relationship we
have with the Holy Spirit. Jesus said, "If ye love me, keep my
commandments. And I will pray the Father, and he shall give you
another Comforter, that he may abide with you for ever …ye know
him; for he dwelleth with you, and shall be in you" (John 14:15–17).
Christ's presence with man changed. We now have the power of
the Holy Spirit, who lives in us and helps us love one another.

Lord, help us to love others as You love us.

41

Notes

Spiritual Gifts

> But the manifestation of the Spirit is given to every
> man to profit withal.
>
> —1 Corinthians 12:7

Spiritual gifts are given to each believer for the purpose of
glorifying God, building up the church, and edifying the body of
Christ. God never promised to build an individual ministry. He
did promise to build His church. The most detailed lists of spiritual
gifts are found in Romans 12, Ephesians 4, and 1 Corinthians
12. They include exhortation, giving, mercy, prophecy, service,
teaching, evangelism, administration, discernment, faith, healing,
knowledge, miracles, tongues, and wisdom. God has equipped
each church—the local body of baptized believers—for several
reasons. "For the perfecting of the saints, for the work of the
ministry, for the edifying of the body of Christ" (Ephesians 4:12).

For the perfecting of the saints, God has uniquely equipped each
believer in the local church. The Holy Spirit will accomplish His
will for each believer. "For we are his workmanship, created in
Christ Jesus unto good works, which God hath before ordained
that we should walk in them" (Ephesians 2:10).

For the work of the ministry, God's mission for the church is very
simple. "Go ye therefore, and teach all nations, baptizing them
in the name of the Father, and of the Son, and of the Holy Ghost:
Teaching them to observe all things whatsoever I have commanded
you" (Matthew 28:19–20).

For the edifying of the body of Christ, the Holy Spirit will
accomplish His will for the edification of each local body. "From
whom the whole body fitly joined together and compacted by that
which every joint supplieth, according to the effectual working in
the measure of every part, maketh increase of the body unto the
edifying of itself in love" (Ephesians 4:16).

Lord, help us to use our spiritual gifts as You desire.

Jesus Wept

Jesus wept.

—John 11:35

"Jesus saith unto her, Said I not unto thee, that, if thou wouldest believe, thou shouldest see the glory of God?" (John 11:40). A superficial reading of John 11 leaves the casual observer with the belief that Jesus was weeping for Lazarus. We know that both Mary and Martha had faith in Jesus. However, during this time of crisis, their understanding of Jesus was questionable. "Then said Martha unto Jesus, Lord, if thou hadst been here, my brother had not died" (v. 21). "Then when Mary was come where Jesus was, and saw him, she fell down at his feet, saying unto him, Lord, if thou hadst been here, my brother had not died" (v. 32). Did their faith limit Jesus? If they truly believed that He was the Christ, why did they not consider that Jesus could raise Lazarus from the dead? Does our faith ever limit the power of God?

I can picture Jesus slowly walking among Mary, Martha, and the Jewish leaders of Bethany. So many who claimed to know God, but failed to see the very presence of God. No wonder "he groaned in the spirit, and was troubled" (v. 33). Yes, Jesus was weeping for the living. There are two reasons we know this.

First, no group on earth ever misread the Lord Jesus like the Jewish leaders. They believed that he was weeping for Lazarus. "Then said the Jews, Behold how he loved him" (v. 36). Second, and probably the most compelling reason: Why would Jesus be weeping for Lazarus, when in a moment, He would be calling him to break death's grip and show forth the glory of God? "He cried with a loud voice, Lazarus, come forth" (v. 43). It took seeing for the multitude to believe: "Then many of the Jews [who] had seen the things which Jesus did, believed on him" (v. 45). Jesus is the resurrection and the life. Believe now and see God work in your life.

Lord, help us see the glory of God.

45

Death and Sin at Calvary

And with him they crucify two thieves; the one on his
right hand, and the other on his left.

—Mark 15:27

Three men died at Calvary. One man died in sin, one man died for
sin, and one man died to sin. The first, a thief, died in sin because
he possessed the natural condition of all men. The second, our
Savior, died for sin after proclaiming the gospel of God for all men.
The last, a thief, died to sin and received salvation as all who trust
in Jesus Christ as Savior.

First, note the thief who died in sin. All men without Christ are
dead in sin. "He that hath the Son hath life; and he that hath not
the Son of God hath not life" (1 John 5:12). "Except a man be
born again, he cannot see the kingdom of God" (John 3:3). It is
imperative that you accept Christ or you will die in your sin and
spend eternity separated from God.

Second, note our Savior, who died for sin. "Christ died for our sins
according to the scriptures" (1 Corinthians 15:3). He died for all
men. "But we see Jesus … that he by the grace of God should taste
death for every man" (Hebrews 2:9). "For even the Son of man
came not to be ministered unto, but to minister, and to give his life
a ransom for many" (Mark 10:45).

Lastly, note the thief who died to sin. This man came to the
realization of who Jesus was and turned to Him in faith. "And
we indeed justly; for we receive the due reward of our deeds: but
this man hath done nothing amiss. And he said unto Jesus, Lord;
remember me when thou comest into thy kingdom" (Luke 23:41–
42). Jesus' response for this man was the same as it has been for all
men throughout history and as it will be until His second coming.
"And Jesus said unto him, Verily I say unto thee, today shalt thou
be with me in paradise" (v. 43).

Lord, thank You that Christ willingly died for us.

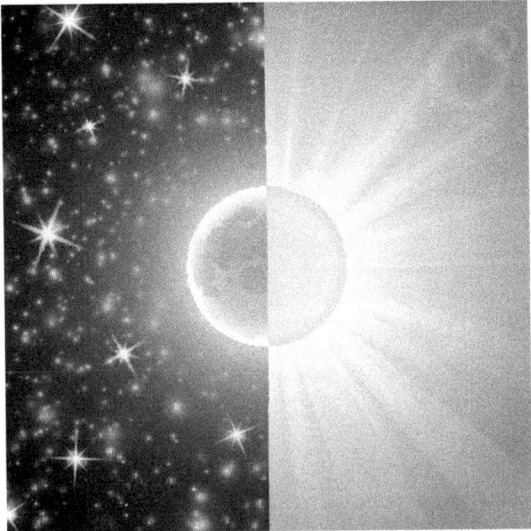

Two Great Lights

> And God made two great lights; the greater light to rule
> the day, and the lesser light to rule the night.
> —Genesis 1:16

The greater light is the sun; the lesser light is the moon. Consider the characteristics of these lights. Simply stated, the sun provides the light and the moon has no light in and of itself. The moon reflects light, and the source of this light is the sun. The lesser light rules in darkness and provides reflected light.

This is symbolic of a Christian's relationship to Jesus Christ. Jesus said, "I am the light of the world; he that followeth me shall not walk in darkness, but shall have the light of life" (John 8:12). Christ is the light of life in the redeemed. God uses this reflected light to point others to Christ. "God is light, and in Him is no darkness at all" (1 John 1:5).

Christians are commanded to share the love of God with the world. The only way that man can share the love of God is with the power of God. Once man has received salvation through the blood of Christ, he is sealed with the Holy Spirit and able to reflect the God of heaven in a dark world. "Ye should show forth the praises of Him who hath called you out of darkness into His marvelous light" (1 Peter 2:9). satan attempts to keep the world in darkness. He controls those who have not accepted Christ and blinds their minds to the truth (light) of God. "In whom the god of this world hath blinded the minds of them which believe not, lest the light of the glorious gospel of Christ, who is the image of God, should shine unto them" (2 Corinthians 4:4).

Christians are the reflected light of Christ. "Let your light so shine before men, that they may see your good works, and glorify your Father, who is in heaven" (Matthew 5:16).

Lord, help us be a light in a dark world, a reflection of You.

49

Notes

Forgiveness—It's Not Forgetting

For I will forgive their iniquity, and I will remember
their sin no more.
—Jeremiah 31:34

I cannot find any Scripture that says that God will forget man's
sin. None. There is a difference between forgetting sin and not
remembering sin. The Scriptures clearly state that God will not
remember sin. "Their sins…will I remember no more" (Hebrews
8:12). "Their sins and iniquities will I remember no more" (10:17).
Since God is omniscient (all-knowing), it is impossible for Him to
forget sin. What is the difference?

This demonstrates God's great love of forgiveness. God's desire is
that those who have trusted Christ as Savior model forgiveness as
the example God has provided. "For if ye forgive … your heavenly
Father will also forgive you: But if ye forgive not … neither will
your Father forgive" (Matthew 6:14–15). God forgives in like
manner. The greatest quality of forgiveness is not remembering
sin. I wish that God would forget my sin, but He does not. The
next best thing is that God does not remember my sin. Once I have
earnestly repented of my sin and sought God's forgiveness, He will
not remember my sin. This means that God will never bring up
that sin again. He has not forgotten the sin, but He has promised
not to remember it or bring it to my memory. Doesn't that really
express the love that our Savior has for us?

This is not so with satan; he uses every opportunity to bring our
sin to our memory. satan will throw our past sin in our face and
cause us to doubt the promises that God has made. We need to be
as forgiving as God. "Therefore, if thou bring thy gift to the altar,
and there rememberest that thy brother hath ought against thee;
Leave there thy gift … go thy way … be reconciled to thy brother"
(Matthew 5:23–24). Forgiving as God has forgiven us implies not
remembering one another's sin.

Lord, help us to forgive others as You have forgiven us.

The Little Foxes

Take us the foxes, the little foxes, that spoil the vines,
for our vines have tender grapes.
—Song of Solomon 2:15

Why does it seem easier to guard against the big foxes? Maybe it is because they are more recognizable. Big foxes call for big fences. If I concentrate on defending against the big foxes, I may become careless with the little foxes (little evils). Scripture constantly reminds me to guard against the little foxes. "Yet a little sleep, a little slumber" (Proverbs 6:10). "Dead flies cause the ointment ... to send forth a stinking savour: so doth a little folly him that is in reputation for wisdom and honour" (Ecclesiastes 10:1). "Know ye not that a little leaven leaveneth the whole lump?" (1 Corinthians 5:6).

Do the little foxes hinder our fellowship with God as much as the big foxes? Maybe more? Is it possible that our tender, less mature fruit is more vulnerable? Consider the fruit outlined in Galatians 5:22–23—specifically love. "We know that we have passed from death unto life, because we love the brethren" (1 John 3:14). For example, if there is dissention in the body of Christ, there is dissention between the brethren. Sometimes rather than deal with difficult people, I ignore them. How does Scripture tell me to deal with them? "Whatsoever ye would that men should do to you, do ye even so to them" (Matthew 7:12).

I should also focus on Christ's commands. Christ's commands include, "Go thee therefore," "Study to shew thyself approved," and "Pray always." Little foxes keep me from being obedient to these commands and might just be my indifference to obeying God's will. "And we have confidence in the Lord touching you, that ye both do and will do the things which we command you" (2 Thessalonians 3:4).

Lord, help us to guard against the little foxes.

Notes

Dumb Faithfulness

> And, behold, thou shalt be dumb, and not able to speak,
> until the day that these things shall be performed.
> —Luke 1:20

The meaning here is not dumb as in "ignorance," but dumb as in "mute." Man often does not understand and frequently questions the providence of God. Zacharias and Elisabeth "were both righteous before God, walking in all the commandments and ordinances of the Lord blameless" (Luke 1:6). Why was this righteous priest struck dumb? Gabriel told Zacharias why he would not be able to speak: "Thou believest not my words, which shall be fulfilled in their season" (v. 20). Could it have been because Zacharias was in the very act of service to God when he demonstrated his unbelief? "That while he executed the priest's office before God" (v. 8). Note two important aspects to God's providence with this story.

First, Zacharias and Elisabeth prayed many years for a son, but God's plan would be fulfilled according to His purpose. Gabriel proclaimed the truth that God would answer their prayers according to His timetable. "Believest not my words, which shall be fulfilled in their season" (v. 20). Ecclesiastes proclaims what this couple experienced. "To everything there is a season, and a time to every purpose under the heaven" (Ecclesiastes 3:1). Second, God gives us the ability to live above our circumstances. By God's will, He will not allow anything to influence our circumstances that by His grace, we cannot overcome.

Too many times I have been absorbed with my circumstances, rather than keeping my focus on Christ. The moment I put my eyes back on the living Christ, the burdens seem to become opportunities to be conformed to the image of His Son.

Lord, help me to be faithful.

Our Father

After this manner therefore pray ye.

—Matthew 6:9

The prayer Jesus instructed us to pray (Matthew 6:9–13) is a model prayer and not necessarily the words we are to repeat over and over. Although innocently we often hear children say the words of the Lord's Prayer, this was not the intent. We know this because of what Jesus said earlier in Matthew: "But when ye pray, use not vain repetitions, as the heathen do" (v. 7).

Jesus' model prayer reveals several important principles. "Our" Father demonstrates that God is the Father of all who repent and that our prayers should be directed to the holy and righteous God of heaven, our Creator. We have a specific relationship to the one to whom we pray, "our Father." We are His children. We should ask that God's presence be with us and His will be done. "Thy kingdom come, Thy will be done in earth, as it is in heaven" (v. 10). We should pray daily, "Give us this day our daily bread" (v. 11). Our need is daily. Daily bread is symbolic of God's provision of manna for the children of Israel in the wilderness. God knows our needs before we ask. Our asking is not for His benefit; it reminds us of our daily need.

Our prayer time should be a time of confession, praise, and petition. "And forgive us our debts, as we forgive our debtors. And lead us not into temptation, but deliver us from evil: For thine is the kingdom, and the power, and the glory, forever. Amen" (vv. 12–13). Confession provides me the opportunity to admit my sin. I should praise God for who He is and not for what He has done for me. He does things for me because He loves me. God does not want praise for His love. God is holy, righteous, and worthy of praise. Petitioning allows me to think about the things that I depend on God for on a daily basis. Protection for loved ones, financial responsibility, a loving spirit, and being an effective witness for Christ are but a few of our daily needs.

Lord, teach us to pray: "Our Father."

Notes

Where Is My Focus

Now Jesus loved Martha, and her sister, and Lazarus.
—John 11:5

The wording differences between verse 1 and verse 5 of John 11 are interesting: "Now a certain man was sick, named Lazarus, of Bethany, the town of Mary and her sister Martha" (John 11:1). Would Mary be disappointed not being recognized by name like Martha? Mary continually maintained a proper focus. Luke records that Mary sat at Jesus' feet and heard His words. This same passage recorded by Luke indicates that Martha's focus was not on the Savior but on the things of the moment. "Martha was cumbered about much serving ... and said, Lord, dost thou not care that my sister hath left me ... bid her therefore that she help me" (Luke 10:40).

On the other hand, Mary demonstrates for us a proper focus on the Savior. "Then took Mary a pound of ointment of spikenard, very costly, and anointed the feet of Jesus, and wiped his feet with her hair" (John 12:3). Having the proper focus, Mary would have never worried about recognition. No doubt, these sisters would have read these passages after John recorded them. Oftentimes, when my focus is not on Jesus, I would possibly question not being recognized. Jesus loved Martha dearly and knew her weaknesses. This is evident in the loving way He rebuked her after she expressed discouragement. "Martha, Martha, thou art careful and troubled about many things: But one thing is needful" (Luke 10:41–42).

Jesus tells us that the one thing that is needful is to keep our focus on Him. "I am come that they might have life, and that they might have it more abundantly" (John 10:10). I can live life more abundantly when I keep my focus on Jesus.

Lord, help us to focus on You.

Notes

Sin Was Not Created

And God saw everything that he had made, and,
behold, it was very good.

—Genesis 1:31

Is sin good? No. Sin cost the life of our Lord and Savior, Jesus
Christ. Since everything God made was very good, He did not
create sin—case closed. Actually, that is not good enough for the
nonbeliever. The skeptic would question this, noting that the Bible
says that God created all things. "By him were all things created ...
all things were created by him" (Colossians 1:16–17).

There is an explanation for sin. Unlike creation where there is
something tangible (something exists), sin is not the presence of
something but the absence of something. This can be illustrated
with several verses. "And God said, Let the earth bring forth
grass ... and the fruit tree yielding fruit ... and it was so" (Genesis
1:11). "And out of the ground made the LORD God to grow every
tree" (2:9). "And the LORD God commanded the man ... But of
the tree of the knowledge of good and evil, thou shalt not eat of
it: for in the day that thou eatest thereof thou shalt surely die"
(2:16–17).

Note the Tree of Knowledge of Good and Evil. Was the Tree of
Knowledge evil? No. Everything God created was very good. It did
not contain good fruit and evil fruit. It became the knowledge of
good and evil for Adam and Eve the moment they disobeyed God
and ate the fruit. Prior to this time, Adam and Eve had only known
good. They acquired the knowledge of evil when they disobeyed
God's command. Sin is not the presence of something, but the
absence of obedience—obedience to a holy God. "Wherefore, as by
one man sin entered into the world, and death by sin; and so death
passed upon all men" (Romans 5:12). Sin entered into the world by
man, not God.

Lord, help us understand that You did not create sin.

Notes

Instruction, Influence, Image

So God created man in his own image, in the image of
God created he him; male and female.

—Genesis 1:27

S. Truett Cathy, founder and CEO of Chick-fil-A restaurants, started his restaurant business in 1946 by opening the Dwarf Grill in Hapeville, Georgia. Chick-fil-A's corporate purpose is, "To glorify God by being a faithful steward of all that is entrusted to us and to have a positive influence on other people who come into contact with Chick-fil-A." Mr. Cathy once said, "Instruction is what you say, influence is what you do, but image is what you are." His assertion is biblically sound.

As Christians, we are to provide instruction using the Word of God. "All scripture is given by inspiration of God, and is profitable for doctrine, for reproof, for correction, for instruction in righteousness" (2 Timothy 3:16). The Bible directs us to listen to the instruction of our parents. "My son, hear the instruction of thy father, and forsake not the law of thy mother" (Proverbs 1:8). Regarding influence, behavior is caught, not taught. "Be thou an example of the believers, in word, in conversation, in charity, in spirit, in faith, in purity" (1 Timothy 4:12). What we do demonstrates if we believe what we say we believe.

Lastly, image is what we are. We are a reflection of God because we were created in the image of God. "And God said, Let us make man in our image" (Genesis 1:26). The world should know that we are different. Being created in God's image was God's design. We should "let [our] light so shine before men" (Matthew 5:16). After all, our light is not our light; it is God's light. What we say is important, what we do is as important, but what we are is the most important. The world should know that we are Christians by what we say, what we do, and who we are.

Lord, help us remember that we are created in Your image.

Notes

What Is Missing

Yet lackest thou one thing.

—Luke 18:22

The rich young ruler had everything the world considers as necessary for being successful in life. He had wealth: "He was very rich" (Luke 18:23). He was young: "The young man" (Matthew 19:20). He was influential: "A certain ruler" (Luke 18:18). Yet this young man came to the Savior because he knew something was missing.

When the young man asked about eternal life, note that Jesus only quoted from what Matthew Henry refers to as the Table II commandments. "Do not commit adultery, Do not kill, Do not steal, Do not bear false witness, Honour thy father and thy mother" (v. 20). Recall that the first four commandments (Table I) deal with man's relationship to God, while the last six commandments (Table II) deal with man's relationship to man.

Jesus spoke to the young man about natural life because he had to move from the natural understanding of trust to the eternal understanding of trust. This eternal understanding involves one's willingness to keep the Table I commandments: "Thou shalt have no other gods before me...Thou shalt not make unto thee any graven image...Thou shalt not take the name of the LORD thy God in vain...Remember the sabbath day, to keep it holy" (Exodus 20:3-8).

Note that there are four Table I commandments, but the young man lacked one thing–the God of heaven. This includes keeping the four Table I commandments. "The natural man receiveth not the things of the Spirit of God: for they are foolishness unto him: neither can he know them, because they are spiritually discerned" (1 Corinthians 2:14). Only by understanding and keeping the Table I commandments, can one properly understand and keep the Table II commandments.

Lord, help us to trust in You as our Savior.

Spiritual Warfare

Be strong in the Lord, and in the power of his might.
—Ephesians 6:10

Being strong in the Lord and in the power of His might requires us to yield any personal power that we think we possess. Just as important to understand is that this type of warfare requires spiritual weapons. Our enemy is not physical, but spiritual. "For we wrestle not against flesh and blood, but against principalities … against spiritual wickedness in high places" (Ephesians 6:12). The good news is that God did not call us to defeat satan. God has already defeated satan in the person of His Son, Jesus Christ. "And you, being dead in your sins … hath he quickened together with him, having forgiven you all trespasses; … nailing it to his cross; And having spoiled principalities and powers … triumphing over them in it" (Colossians 2:13–15). The victory has already been won.

However, we do battle. Being strong in the power of His might includes the equipping of the redeemed with God's armor. "Wherefore take unto you the whole armour of God that ye may be able to withstand in the evil day" (Ephesians 6:13). To gird our loins about with truth (v. 14) means to be ready, and to be ready with the truth. Jesus said that He is the way, the truth, and the life. Be ready with Christ. The breastplate of righteousness protects the most critical body part, the heart. Having our feet shod with the preparation of the gospel helps us to "stand" against the enemy, standing with the gospel. The shield of faith and helmet of salvation protects us from unsuspecting blows from the enemy. The sword of the Spirit (Word of God) equips us with the truth of the gospel to help pierce the hard hearts of those who have yet to accept Christ as Savior. Prayer permits an avenue of communication with almighty God, enabling us to persevere against the enemy.

Lord, in Your power, help us to overcome evil.

Notes

Jehovah Shalom

> Then Gideon built an altar there unto the Lord, and
> called it Jehovah-shalom.
>
> —Judges 6:24

The book of Judges records an unfortunate repeated pattern in the life of God's chosen people: sin, judgment, repentance, and forgiveness. God used selected individuals (judges) to lead Israel back to Him. Once when the children of Israel were in sin, God chose to deliver them into the hands of the Midianites for seven long years. "They came as grasshoppers... Israel was greatly impoverished because of the Midianites" (Judges 6:5–6).

Gideon was God's chosen instrument for Israel's deliverance from the Midianites. Gideon questioned God about his (Gideon's) ability to deliver God's people. God's reply was encouraging: "Surely I will be with thee, and thou shalt smite the Midianites as one man" (Judges 6:16). When God delivered as promised, Gideon dedicated an altar built for Him and called it Jehovah-shalom. Gideon found peace in God, as we should. Our Lord's promises to continually be with us can be found throughout the Scriptures, including, "For he hath said, I will never leave thee, nor forsake thee" (Hebrews 13:5).

The noun form of *shalom* comes from the root word *shalem*, meaning "to be complete" or "whole." *Shalom* occurs over 250 times in the Old Testament. While the most common usage of *shalom* today is that of a greeting, in Old Testament times, it was used more often as a term for good relationships and refers to "peace with God." This peace is a gift from God.

God's peace is often found in the context of covenants as with such passages found in Numbers. "The LORD bless thee, and keep thee: The LORD make his face shine upon thee, and be gracious unto thee: The LORD lift up his countenance upon thee, and give thee peace" (Numbers 6:24–26).

Lord, help us to live and understand Your peace.

Notes

See

> And the LORD said unto Joshua, See …
>
> —Joshua 6:2

Have you ever had someone say to you, "I told you so"? A polite way of saying that is to say, "See."

The Lord had advised others about demonstrating faith and then seeing the glory of God. "Jesus saith unto her, Said I not unto thee, that, if thou wouldest believe, thou shouldest see the glory of God?" (John 11:40).

What did Joshua see? Joshua saw that Jericho was straitly shut up because of the children of Israel. Joshua saw what the mighty men of valor of Jericho saw. They saw the priests bearing the ark of the covenant before the people. They saw "the feet of the priests that bare the ark were dipped in the brim of the water … That the waters which came down from above stood and rose up upon a heap…and the people passed over right against Jericho" (Joshua 3:14–16).

The mighty men of valor of Jericho saw the mighty hand of the living God. They reported this to the king and citizens of Jericho. What was the result of this report? Fear was rampant. "When all the kings of the Amorites, … on the side of Jordan westward, and all the kings of the Canaanites, which were by the sea, heard that the LORD had dried up the waters of Jordan from before the children of Israel, until we were passed over, that their heart melted, neither was there spirit in them any more" (Joshua 5:1).

The children of Israel were soon to see God Himself work another miracle. "And ye shall compass the city, all ye men of war, and go round about the city once. Thus shalt thou do six days" (Joshua 6:3). "Shout; for the LORD hath given you the city" (v. 16). When we step out on faith, we will see too.

Lord, help us to see.

The Cross Was Not in the Cup

O my Father, if it be possible, let this cup pass from me:
nevertheless not as I will, but as thou wilt.
—Matthew 26:39

I have heard some speculate that during these moments in the garden, Christ was requesting of God an alternative to the cross. Was there another way to redeem the world without the cross? Absolutely not. "Therefore doth my Father love me, because I lay down my life ... No man taketh it from me ... I have power to lay it down, and I have power to take it again. This commandment have I received of my Father" (John 10:17–18). Since Christ had the power granted by the Father to lay His life down and take it up, He would not make such a request?

What was in the cup? Could it be symbolic of the cup referred to in Revelation? "The same shall drink of the wine of the wrath of God, which is poured out...into the cup of his indignation" (Revelation 14:10). "Babylon came in remembrance before God, to give unto her the cup of the wine of the fierceness of his wrath" (16:19). What about the cup that Christ mentions in Mark? "But Jesus said unto them, ye know not what ye ask: can ye drink of the cup that I drink of?" (Mark 10:38).

The wages of sin is death. This has to be the cup that all lost men and women will drink. It contains the wrath of God. It will contain suffering, punishment, and judgment for all who reject Christ. Christ was the acceptable sacrifice—blameless, without sin. But for our sakes, He willingly drank from this cup. Christ had to suffer, become sin, and be slain to provide redemption.

Christ's suffering is mentioned in many Scripture passages. "He is despised and rejected of men; a man of sorrows, and acquainted with grief" (Isaiah 53:3). "The Son of man must suffer many things" (Luke 9:22). "He was bruised for our iniquities ... and with his stripes we are healed" (Isaiah 53:5).

Lord, help us to understand that Christ suffered for us.

Notes

Togetherness

> And the LORD God said, it is not good that the man
> should be alone.
>
> —Genesis 2:18

God's purpose for our lives includes others. Togetherness is the
key for Christian citizenship. Being faithful to Christ includes
believing and belonging. "So we, being many, are one body in
Christ, and every one members one of another" (Romans 12:5).

We are joined together. "The whole body fitly joined together …
according to the effectual working in the measure of every
part … unto the edifying of itself in love" (Ephesians 4:16). We
are knit together. "That their hearts might be comforted, being
knit together… to the acknowledgement of the mystery of God …
and of Christ" (Colossians 2:2). We assemble together. "Not
forsaking the assembling of ourselves together, as the manner
of some is; but exhorting one another … as ye see the day
approaching" (Hebrews 10:25).

We labor together. "For we are laborers together with God: ye
are God's husbandry, ye are God's building" (1 Corinthians 3:9).
We are comforted together. "For where two or three are gathered
together in my name, there am I in the midst of them" (Matthew
18:20). We rejoice together. "That both he that soweth and he that
reapeth may rejoice together" (John 4:36).

We will be caught up together. "Then we which are alive and
remain shall be caught up together with them in the clouds, to
meet the Lord in the air: and so shall we ever be with the Lord"
(1 Thessalonians 4:17). We will be glorified together. "And if
children, then heirs; heirs of God, and joint-heirs with Christ; if so
be that we suffer with him, that we may be also glorified together"
(Romans 8:17). We will live together with Him. "Who died for us,
that, whether we wake or sleep, we should live together with him"
(1 Thessalonians 5:10).

Lord, thank you for clarifying the meaning of togetherness.

Proof That God Exists

For the invisible things of him from the creation of the
world are clearly seen, being understood by the things
that are made, even his eternal power and Godhead; so
that they are without excuse.

—Romans 1:20

Have you ever heard someone say that you cannot prove that God
exists? Actually, the truth that God exists is found right in God's
Word, and this proof is all around us. Romans 1:20 says that the
invisible things of God are clearly seen and understood by the things
that are made. Consider the things that are made. God made the
heaven (firmament) and the earth (dry land), the light, the waters
(seas), the grass, trees, fruit, day, night, seasons, days, years, sun,
moon, stars, fowls, the fish, cattle—every living creature. And most
importantly, He made humankind. "I am fearfully and wonderfully
made" (Psalm 139:14). The things that are made are clearly seen on a
daily basis. Walk under the trees, beside a lake, or walk in the waves
of the ocean. Sit still and listen to the birds and feel the cool of the
evening breeze. Gaze into the evening sky and attempt to count the
endless number of stars. "By the word of the Lord were the heavens
made; and all the host of them by the breath of his mouth" (Psalm
33:6). "All things were made by him; and without him was not
anything made that was made" (John 1:3). "The heavens declare the
glory of God; and the firmament sheweth his handywork" (Psalm
19:1). Yes–The proof is all around us.

The things that are clearly seen also provide us with the
understanding of His eternal power and Godhead. His eternal
power, because His power is unlike any other. His Godhead
(Trinity), because we receive understanding about God the Father,
God the Son, and God the Holy Spirit. Yes, this proof is all around
us. God's Word says that we are without excuse. Everyone will
stand before God one day and confess this understanding that is so
clearly seen–all around us.

Lord, help us to understand that we are all without excuse.

Notes

Looking Forward, Looking Up

I will lift up mine eyes unto the hills, from whence
cometh my help.

—Psalm 121:1

Have you ever heard the saying, "Keep your chin up"? This saying
is scriptural, and it is God's desire for the redeemed.

Consider looking forward. "And Jesus said unto him, No man,
having put his hand to the plough, and looking back, is fit for the
kingdom of God" (Luke 9:62). There are two key lessons in this
verse. First, once we have been redeemed, we should never go back
to those sinful habits for which God has forgiven us. Figuratively,
looking back indicates that we really haven't given up the old
life. "If any man be in Christ, he is a new creature: old things are
passed away ... all things are become new" (2 Corinthians 5:17).
Old things are passed away—don't look back. Second, we can rest
assured that once God has forgiven us, He will not remember our
sin anymore. "For I will forgive their iniquity, and I will remember
their sin no more" (Jeremiah 31:34). God will never throw our old
sins back in our face.

Consider looking up. "I will lift up mine eyes unto the hills, from
whence cometh my help" (Psalm 121:1). Keeping our chins up
requires us to lift our eyes up. But why does the psalmist say, "lift
up mine eyes unto the hills"? Anyone who has ever lived around
the base of a mountain range or hills knows this. When the rains
come, those areas near the base of the hills receive the most water.
The water landing on the slopes comes down like rivers of living
water. "For as the rain cometh down, and ... watereth the earth ...
So shall my word be that goeth forth out of my mouth: ... it shall
accomplish that which I please" (Isaiah 55:10–11). We can count on
God's Word to help us keep looking forward and looking up.

Lord, help us to keep looking forward and looking up.

Love—Greater Than Faith and Hope

And now abideth faith, hope, charity [love], these
three; but the greatest of these is charity.
—1 Corinthians 13:13

How can love be greater than faith and hope? After all, there
are a number of Bible verses that demonstrate the importance
of faith and hope. "For therein is the righteousness of God
revealed from faith to faith ... The just shall live by faith"
(Romans 1:17). "But without faith it is impossible to please him:
for he that cometh to God must believe ... that he is a rewarder
of them that diligently seek him" (Hebrews 11:6). "Hope thou in
God" (Psalm 42:11). "Now the God of hope fill you with all joy
and peace" (Romans 15:13).

First Corinthians 13, otherwise known as the "great love chapter,"
begins by emphasizing the importance and priority of love.
"Though I have the gift of prophecy, and understand all mysteries,
and all knowledge; and though I have all faith ... and have not
charity [love], I am nothing" (1 Corinthians 13:2).

Why is love greater than faith and hope? Before faith and hope,
there was the great I Am. "God is love" (1 John 4:8). God does not
merely demonstrate the characteristics of love; love is the very
essence of God's nature. He suffers long with those He loves. God
is kind. He does not envy, nor is He boastful or prideful. He is
longsuffering and not easily provoked. God never thinks any evil
and certainly does not rejoice in iniquity. God only rejoices in the
truth. Most importantly, God never fails.

God's love existed long before our faith in Jesus Christ. "Looking
unto Jesus the author and finisher of our faith" (Hebrews 12:2).
God's love existed long before all of our hopes and dreams.
Because God's love is the foundation of our faith and hope, love is
greater than faith and hope. God is love.

Lord, help us understand Your love.

The Inescapable Question

What shall I do then with Jesus which is called Christ?
—Matthew 27:22

This is the key question in life that everyone must ask. Pilate confronted himself with this question. If you have not accepted Jesus Christ as your personal Savior, ask yourself this question. Do not wash your hands of this moment to experience the love of God and accept Christ as your Lord and Savior. "Who is this?" (Matthew 21:10). Many people in all walks of life have wondered this about Jesus. He is "the way, the truth, and the life" (John 14:6). "For there is one God, and one mediator between God and men, the man Christ Jesus; who gave himself a ransom for all" (1 Timothy 2:5–6).

Jesus is the only way for man to be reconciled to God and receive eternal life. Who will ask you to wonder about this truth? Jesus Himself. He caused the Pharisees to wonder. "What think ye of Christ? whose son is he?" (Matthew 22:42). He caused the disciples to wonder. "Whom do men say that I the Son of man am?" (v. 16:13). "But whom say ye that I am?" (v. 15). Peter knew who Jesus was. "And Simon Peter answered and said, Thou art the Christ, the Son of the living God" (v. 16). Now that you know who Jesus is, ask yourself, What shall I do then with Jesus? You are a few moments away from eternal life. This life does not start in the future; it can start today. Do something with Jesus. "If thou shalt confess with thy mouth the Lord Jesus, and shalt believe in thine heart that God hath raised him from the dead, thou shalt be saved" (Romans 10:9).

Pray a prayer similar to the following: "Dear God, I know that Jesus is Your Son, and that He died on the cross and was raised from the dead. I know I have sinned and need forgiveness. I am willing to turn from my sins and receive Jesus as my Savior and Lord. Thank You for saving me. In Jesus' name, Amen."

Lord, help us to share what we should do with Jesus.

Notes

God's G.R.A.C.E.

For by grace are ye saved through faith; and that not of
yourselves: it is the gift of God.
—Ephesians 2:8

You can share the gospel by remembering a few familiar verses.

G. Gift (Eternal life is a free gift.) Eternal life is a free gift, you
cannot earn it. "For by grace are ye saved through faith; and that
not of yourselves: it is the *gift* of God: Not of works, lest any man
should boast" (Ephesians 2:8–9). "For the wages of sin is death;
but the *gift* of God is eternal life through Jesus Christ our Lord"
(Romans 6:23). Gifts are not earned through works.

R. Repent (Everyone is a sinner.) Man must turn to God for
eternal life. "Except ye repent, ye shall all likewise perish" (Luke
13:3). "For all have sinned" (Romans 3:23).

A. Almighty God (God loves you.) "For God so loved the world,
that he gave his only begotten Son, that whosoever believeth in
him should not perish, but have everlasting life" (John 3:16). God is
also a just God. "There is no God else beside me; a just God and a
Savior" (Isaiah 45:21).

C. Christ (Jesus willingly died for you.) Jesus is the only way.
"Jesus saith to him, I am the way, the truth, and the life: no man
cometh unto the Father; but by me" (John 14:6). "For there is one
God, and one mediator between God and men, the man Christ
Jesus" (1 Timothy 2:5–6). There is no other way.

E. Express (Each person must accept Jesus Christ.) "If thou shalt
confess with thy mouth the Lord Jesus, and shalt believe in thine
heart that God hath raised him from the dead, thou shalt be saved"
(Romans 10:9). "For whosoever shall call upon the name of the
Lord shall be saved" (v. 13).

Lord, help us to share the gospel faithfully.

Notes

Are You Persuaded?

I know whom I have believed, and am persuaded that
he is able.

—2 Timothy 1:12

The two blind men were persuaded. "Two blind men followed
him…saying…have mercy on us… Jesus saith unto them, Believe
ye that I am able to do this? They said unto him, Yea, Lord. Then
touched he their eyes, saying, According to your faith be it unto
you. And their eyes were opened" (Matthew 9:27–30). The rich
young ruler was not persuaded. "Go and sell that thou hast, and
give to the poor … come and follow me. But when the young man
heard that … he went away sorrowful" (Matthew 19:21–22). Yes, he
went away sorrowful.

Peter was persuaded. "But whom say ye that I am? And Simon
Peter answered and said, Thou art the Christ, the Son of the living
God" (Matthew 16:15–16). Thomas was not persuaded, until after
the fact.

> But Thomas … said…Except I shall see in his
> hands the print of the nails … and thrust my hand
> into his side, I will not believe. And after eight
> days…then came Jesus … saith he to Thomas,
> Reach hither thy finger, and behold my hands…
> and thrust it into my side: and be not faithless, but
> believing. And Thomas answered and said unto
> him, My LORD and my God.
> —John 20:24–28

The woman with the issue of blood was persuaded. "She came
trembling…she declared unto him…how she was healed
immediately" (Luke 8:47).

Are you persuaded? Do not be like Thomas. Have faith and believe.
You will see the miraculous works of God today.

Lord, help us to be live persuaded.

Offer So Willingly

But who am I, and what is my people, that we should
be able to offer so willingly after this sort? for all things
come of thee, and of thine own have we given thee.
—1 Chronicles 29:14

King David provides an amazing testimony in this passage
regarding the key principles of offerings. These key principles
include affection, affirmation, and ability.

Affection: If we first set our affections on God, this prepares our
hearts to offer so willingly. "Because I have set my affection to
the house of my God, I have of mine own proper good ... which I
have given to the house of my God, over and above all that I have
prepared for the holy house" (1 Chronicles 29:3). It starts with a
proper affection on God.

Affirmation: Affirming who God is helps us understand God's
ownership of all things. "Thine, O LORD, is the greatness, and the
power, and the glory, and the victory, and the majesty: for all that
is in the heaven and in the earth is thine; thine is the kingdom, O
LORD" (v. 11).

Ability: Our ability to offer is provided directly from God. "But
who am I, and what is my people, that we should be able to offer so
willingly after this sort? for all things come of thee, and of thine
own have we given thee" (v. 14).

"As for me, in the uprightness of mine heart I have willingly
offered all these things" (v. 17). "Then the people rejoiced, for that
they offered willingly, because with perfect heart they offered
willingly to the LORD: and David the king also rejoiced with
great joy" (v. 9). When we offer so willingly to God, we are actually
offering what God has provided to us.

Lord, help us to offer so willingly—out of Your hand.

Suffer the Little Children

Jesus said, Suffer little children, and forbid them not, to
come unto me: for of such is the kingdom of heaven.
—Matthew 19:14

Jesus loves children. Several years ago, I experienced the most
difficult time I have ever faced in Christian ministry. I was advised
that close friends of ours had received news that their infant son
was diagnosed with spinal muscular atrophy (SMA). The dad
advised me that God had given them peace about this situation
and it was going to be okay. I went to minister to this young
couple, but I became the object of ministry. After we spoke, I had
the opportunity to visit at this little one's bedside. Dad lowered the
bedside protector and I was able to love him as if he were my own.
I put my cheek against his little forehead and felt his warmth. I
ran my fingers through his hair and his little blue eyes met mine.
It was difficult for me to tell that anything was wrong. Dad tickled
his chin and he shared a cute little smile. I reached to touch his
hand and he gripped my finger. I watched his little tummy, and his
erratic breathing brought back the reality of this dreadful disease.

As I traveled home that evening, I continually lifted him up in
prayer hoping that the Lord would heal him. I notified several
friends the next day and asked for prayer for the family. I expressed
to my family how my heart was so heavy for this young couple
and their son. I just could not shake the thought of those little blue
eyes. When I awoke on Saturday morning, I began thinking again
about the decision his mom and dad would be considering in just a
few hours. The Lord took him home.

I then pictured Jesus Himself holding this little one, and
remembered what his dad had shared with me a couple of days
before. It was going to be okay.

Lord, help us to understand Your mysterious will.

Notes

Sin, Righteousness, and Judgment

And when he is come, he will reprove the world of sin,
and of righteousness, and of judgment.

—John 16:8

The world needs reproving today. The Greek word for *reprove* here means "to convict." It is a legal term used in a similar way as when a prosecuting attorney presents evidence to win a conviction. This is the evidence that the Holy Spirit uses to bring about conviction in the hearts of men. In other words, the world is reproved and those targeted by this evidence are the lost.

The Holy Spirit presents the evidence "of sin, because they believe not on me" (John 16:9). This is the sin of unbelief. Sin is the faithless rebellion of creatures against the just authority of their Creator. This reproof is initiated by our Creator because "there is none that seeketh after God" (Romans 3:11).

The Holy Spirit presents the evidence "of righteousness, because I go to my Father, and ye see me no more" (John 16:10). It is not only important for man to understand his sin but to understand Christ's righteousness and His death as payment for our sin.

Lastly, the Holy Spirit presents the evidence "of judgment, because the prince of this world is judged" (v. 11). In this verse, judgment is pronounced and merely declared. The world is not on trial here; the world has already been judged and found guilty. The world and everyone who has not accepted Christ as Savior is waiting on death row. Christ has already paid the price of that judgment (wages of sin).

Only when we understand our sin as revealed by the Holy Spirit, Christ's righteousness, and God's judgment can we come to a saving knowledge of Jesus Christ. Trust in Him today.

Lord, help us to deliver this message to a lost world.

Notes

He Is Able

He is able.

—2 Timothy 1:12

Jesus is able. In this same verse, Paul states, "He is able to keep that which I have committed unto him against that day" (2 Timothy 1:12). This means that Paul demonstrated his faith in Christ until the Day of Judgment. "Who shall change our vile body, that it may be fashioned like unto his glorious body, according to the working whereby he is able even to subdue all things unto himself" (Philippians 3:21). In the twinkling of an eye, God will fashion us after the Lord Jesus Himself.

"Now unto him that is able to keep you from falling and to present you faultless before the presence of his glory with exceeding joy" (Jude v. 24). Christ not only allows me to stand redeemed before God with His imputed righteousness, but He is able to keep me from falling in this world. "And God is able to make all grace abound toward you; that ye, always having all sufficiency in all things, may abound to every good work" (2 Corinthians 9:8). Oh, how we are blessed. All grace abounds toward us. He is able to provide all sufficiency in all things. "For in that he himself hath suffered being tempted, he is able to succour [to aid] them that are tempted" (Hebrews 2:18). It is also true that God will not suffer us to be tempted above that which we are able to resist.

From a salvation perspective, "he is able also to save them to the uttermost that come unto God by him, seeing he ever liveth to make intercession for them" (Hebrews 7:25). God has more than demonstrated His love toward us. He is willing to save all who come unto Him by Christ Jesus. Jesus lives to make intercession for us. "Now unto him that is able to do exceeding abundantly above all that we ask or think" (Ephesians 3:20). Yes, God is able.

Lord, reassure us to know that You are able.

The Only Begotten

> For God so loved the world, that he gave his only
> begotten Son.
>
> —John 3:16

John 3:16 is one of the most frequently quoted verses in the Bible. "For God so loved the world, that he gave his only begotten Son." Along with John 1:14, they clearly indicate that Jesus was begotten of God: "And we beheld his glory, the glory as of the only begotten of the Father."

What does *begotten* mean? Strong defines *beget* as "to father."[3] Was man begotten? No. Man was created. "And God said; Let us make man in our image, after our likeness" (Genesis 1:26). In his book *Mere Christianity*, C. S. Lewis said,

> When you beget, you beget something of the same kind as yourself. A man begets human babies, a beaver begets little beavers… But when you make, you make something of a different kind from yourself. A bird makes a nest, a beaver builds a dam, a man … may make something more like himself than a wireless set: say, a statue. If he is a clever enough carver he may make a statue which is very like a man … But, of course, it is not a real man. *What God begets is God*; just as what man begets is man. What God creates is not God; just as what man makes is not man."[4] (emphasis added)

This helps us understand the deity of Jesus Christ. Jesus said, "My sheep hear my voice, and I know them … And I give unto them eternal life … I and my Father are one" (John 10:27–30). Only God gives eternal life. "Whosoever believeth in him should not perish, but have everlasting life" (3:16). The Trinity includes God the Father, God the Son, and God the Holy Spirit.

Lord, thank You for helping us understand the deity of Christ.

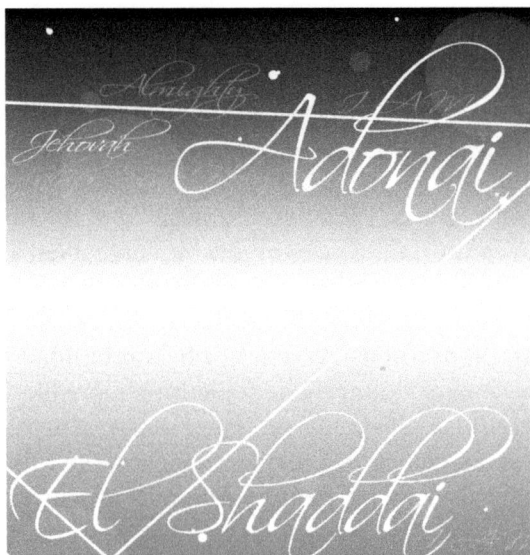

The Names of God

O Lord our Lord, how excellent is thy name in all the
earth.

—Psalm 8:9

Old Testament names had associated meanings as well as revealing
one's identity. God often revealed Himself through His names and
typically they revealed His identity and nature.

"He restoreth my soul: he leadeth me in the paths of righteousness
for his name's sake" (Psalm 23:3). "Therefore for thy name's sake
lead me, and guide me" (31:3). "For our heart shall rejoice in him,
because we have trusted in his holy name" (33:21). Several of God's
Old Testament names include:

El Shaddai: Lord God Almighty
El Elyon: The Most High God
Adonai: Lord, Master
Yahweh: Lord, Jehovah
Jehovah Nissi: The Lord My Banner
Jehovah-Raah: The Lord My Shepherd
Jehovah Rapha: The Lord Who Heals
Jehovah Shammah: The Lord Is There
Jehovah Tsidkenu: The Lord Our Righteousness
Jehovah Mekoddishkem: The Lord Who Sanctifies You
El Olam: The Everlasting God
Elohim: God
Qanna: Jealous
Jehovah Jireh: The Lord Will Provide
Jehovah Shalom: The Lord Is Peace
Jehovah Sabaoth: The Lord of Hosts

God is the Almighty, our Banner, our Shepherd, and our Healer.
He is righteous, everlasting, and jealous. He is our Provider and
our Peace.

Lord, You have such excellent and honorable names.

Notes

Joseph—the King of Wait

And it came to pass at the end of two full years.
—Genesis 41:1

Are you waiting on the Lord for something? Has this waiting caused you disappointment or even bitterness towards God?

Joseph's life was full of waiting. Most of his waiting was due to unfairness. Jacob loved Joseph more than his other children and his brothers hated him. Joseph shared his dreams and they hated him even more. His brothers saw him wearing his coat of many colors and they conspired to slay him. They cast him into a pit, and there Joseph waited. He was then taken captive and sold.

Joseph waited in captivity in the house of Potiphar. Potiphar was an officer of Pharaoh and the captain of the guard. Joseph soon became overseer of all that Potiphar had. The Lord blessed the Egyptian's house for Joseph's sake. When Joseph did not give in to Potiphar's wife, she lied, causing him to be cast into prison.

Joseph then waited in prison. While in prison, Joseph was asked to interpret the dreams of the chief butler and chief baker who had also been cast into prison. After Joseph interpreted these dreams, he spent another two full years in prison before the Lord allowed him to interpret a dream for Pharaoh. What is so remarkable is that there is no evidence in Scripture that Joseph was ever bitter for what his brothers had caused. "But as for you, ye thought evil against me; But God meant it unto good, to bring to pass, as it is this day" (Genesis 50:20).

Joseph's patient waiting proved that "they that wait upon the Lord shall renew their strength; they shall mount up with wings as eagles; they shall run, and not be weary; and they shall walk, and not faint" (Isaiah 40:31). His waiting was comforted with peace.

Lord, help us to wait patiently on You.

Notes

Remember

That no man should be moved by these afflictions: for
yourselves know that we are appointed thereunto.
—1 Thessalonians 3:3

On September 11 every year, we remember the unprecedented
terrorist attacks against our country. We remember as we watched
the videos of airplanes flying directly into the World Trade Center
twin towers in New York City.

We remember the explosions. We remember the faces of the
terrified New Yorkers as they looked up at the billowing smoke
pouring from the twin towers. We remember images of those who
chose to jump. We remember the hundreds of firefighters and
police officers as they attempted to provide order in the midst of
chaos. We remember when the towers imploded. We remember
the destruction at the Pentagon and recount the loss of life. We
remember as we looked at a scorched field in Pennsylvania, a flight
cut short of its certain destination to Washington, DC.

Unlike 9/11 in 2001, when church pews swelled to capacity, most
Americas choose now to recount that year's events from their
homes. This year, there were no reports about church attendance
hitting all-time highs. We only seem to remember the tragic events
of 9/11, rather than remembering God who brought us through it.

God would have us remember Him, His promises, and His
comfort. "In me ye might have peace. In the world ye shall have
tribulation: but be of good cheer; I have overcome the world" (John
16:33). "The Lord GOD will wipe away tears from off all faces"
(Isaiah 25:8). Remember, the Lord is aware of our afflictions, and
He is with us in the midst of our suffering and tragedy.

Lord, help us remember You are with us in all circumstances.

Notes

Trust, Delight, Commit

Trust in the LORD; Delight thyself also in the LORD;
Commit thy way unto the LORD.

—Psalm 37:3–5

Life's encounters are not happenstance. "The steps of a good man
are ordered by the LORD" (Psalm 37:23). Spending quiet time in
God's Word and in prayer at the beginning of each day quiets a
restless heart. This quiet time affords the Lord the opportunity to
reveal His will to us on a daily basis. Too many times, we rush into
our busy day without as much as thanking God for our very breath
of life. God desires that we draw near to Him. "Draw nigh to God,
and he will draw nigh to you" (James 4:8). We draw near to God in
several ways.

First, "**Trust** in the LORD, and do good" (Psalm 37:3). We all
trust in something. What will we choose to trust in today? Walk
circumspectly, trusting Christ to guide us by the Holy Spirit. God
is faithful; He will guide us moment by moment.

Second, "**Delight** thyself also in the LORD" (v. 4). Enjoy the day
that the Lord hath made. God's delight is that we delight in Him.
God is faithful; He shall give thee the desires of thine heart. Look
around at His creation, delight in life.

Third, "**Commit** thy way unto the LORD; trust also in him" (v. 5).
What will we choose to commit to today? God is faithful; and He
shall bring it to pass. Commit to His will today.

God's plan is for us to lead a lost and dying world to His Son, Jesus
Christ. His plan is for the world to see Christ in us. God's desire
is for us to be the light of the world. "Ye are the light of the world"
(Matthew 5:14). That light is Christ's light. The only way to succeed
at God's plan for our life is to trust, delight, and commit to Him
daily.

Lord, help us to trust, delight, and commit to You daily.

Notes

God's Will for My Personal Life

> Let integrity and uprightness preserve me: for I wait
> on thee.
>
> —Psalm 25:21

The most important aspect of the Christian life is that we live with integrity. "The just man walketh in his integrity" (Proverbs 20:7). It is critical for man to understand that he may be able to fool men, but he will never fool an omniscient God. "For nothing is secret... neither anything hid" (Luke 8:17). We will all give an account of ourselves to God. "So then every one of us shall give an account of himself to God" (Romans 14:12). How do we walk in integrity? Never lie, cheat, or steal. God hates a lying tongue. "Lying lips are abomination to the Lord: but they that deal truly are his delight" (Proverbs 12:22). Walk in integrity.

Another key aspect of the Christian life is our speech. We should be able to control our tongues if Christ is Lord. "Let no corrupt communication proceed out of your mouth" (Ephesians 4:29). If the Holy Spirit is in control of our tongues, we would never say an unkind word and we would never participate in or repeat any form of gossip. "For out of the abundance of the heart the mouth speaketh" (Matthew 12:34).

The two most important activities God desires for my personal life are Bible study and personal prayer time. "Study to shew thyself approved unto God, a workman that needeth not to be ashamed, rightly dividing the word of truth" (2 Timothy 2:15).

God's Word is His personal love letter to every Christian. "This book of the law shall not depart out of thy mouth" (Joshua 1:8). Jesus desires us to pray: "And when thou prayest" (Matthew 6:5). Most importantly, we should "pray without ceasing" (1 Thessalonians 5:17). God's will for my personal life includes diligent and dedicated Bible study complemented by a healthy and daily personal prayer time.

Lord, help us to diligently seek Your will.

Faith in God Is Not Blind Faith

I and the lad will go yonder and worship, and come
again to you.

—Genesis 22:5

They had traveled three days before Abraham saw the place
afar off. The two young men with Abraham and Isaac probably
wondered why Abraham stopped and gazed into the distance.
There it was–Mount Moriah. Only one of the travelers—
Abraham—knew why God had commanded this journey.

Blind faith has been defined as stepping out on a belief without first
knowing or seeing the result. Vine defines *faith* as "a conviction
based on hearing."[5] Abraham was most confident when he boldly
proclaimed that he and Isaac would "go yonder and worship, and
come again." What did Abraham know? Abraham knew and
understood God's promise. "For in Isaac shall thy seed be called"
(Genesis 21:12). This could have only meant one of two things for
Abraham. It either meant that when he sacrificed Isaac as the Lord
commanded, God would raise him from the dead, or that the Lord
would intervene and provide a substitute as the sacrifice. Either
way, Abraham knew he would return to the two young men with
Isaac. What faith.

As Christians, we can live this type of faith because we have
received God's promises. "Whereby are given unto us exceeding
great and precious promises: that by these ye might be partakers
of the divine nature" (2 Peter 1:4). Our walk of faith is empowered
by God Himself. "For it is God which worketh in you both to will
and to do of his good pleasure" (Philippians 2:13). Christians can
demonstrate faith by exercising the power of God to will and to do
of His good pleasure. Other promises are "Call unto me, and I will
answer thee, and shew thee … mighty things, which thou knowest
not" (Jeremiah 33:3), and "I will never leave thee, nor forsake thee"
(Hebrews 13:5).

Lord, increase our faith.

Notes

God's Will for My Family

And thou shalt write them upon the posts of thy house,
and on thy gates.

—Deuteronomy 6:9

It is my responsibility to keep the knowledge of God before my family at every possible moment. The head of the household will define the importance of God within the household. This is true whether the head of the household is a man or a woman.

Husbands and wives must understand that "the head of every man is Christ; and the head of the woman is the man; and the head of Christ is God" (1 Corinthians 11:3). Husbands should love their wives "even as Christ also loved the church, and gave himself for it … So ought men to love their wives as their own bodies … [And each should] so love his wife even as himself" (Ephesians 5:25, 28, 33). Wives should "submit yourselves unto your own husbands, as unto the Lord … The wife [should] see that she reverence her husband" (Ephesians 5:22, 33). If men and women would understand this kind of devotion prior to marriage, there would be fewer divorces.

Children should "obey your parents in the Lord: for this is right. Honour thy father and mother; which is the first commandment with promise; that it may be well with thee, and thou mayest live long on the earth" (Ephesians 6:1–3). God tells us that honoring our parents equals long life. Fathers and mothers should "train up a child in the way he should go: and when he is old, he will not depart from it" (Proverbs 22:6). "Fathers, provoke not your children to wrath: but bring them up in the nurture and admonition of the Lord" (Ephesians 6:4). Parents must live the Christian life every moment of every day. We must forever keep the truths of God before our children. "Talk of them when thou sittest in thine house, and when thou walkest by the way, and when thou liest down, and when thou risest up" (Deuteronomy 6:7).

Lord, help us live rightly as families.

Notes

The Keys to the Prodigal

And he said unto him, Son, thou art ever with me, and
all that I have is thine.

—Luke 15:31

Understanding the parable of the prodigal son requires an
understanding of the key characters in the parable: the father and
the two sons. But remember that the storyteller is Jesus, the Son.

Consider the father. The father allowed his younger son to choose
a path he would soon learn to hate. Christians are not puppets.
While God the Father knows what's best for us, He still provides
us with the right to choose. Consider the father's love. The father
patiently watched and waited for his son's return. When he was
a great way off, his father saw him and had compassion; he ran
to his son. The father demanded the best robe, a ring, shoes, and
the fattened calf. Consider the father's forgiveness. He willingly
accepted his son when he returned, and he restored him.

Consider the elder son. He remained steadfast to the father.
However, at the time of his brother's return, he was more
concerned with himself and his faithful acts than his brother's
return. Consider the rebellious younger son. He desired his worldly
inheritance, thinking it would bring him happiness. He soon
discovered what many of us learn when we are rebellious. If we
desire to leave the Father's watchful care, we will soon become
as the world and eat with the swine. When this wayward son
understood and determined that he truly wanted to return to his
father, the father welcomed him with open arms, forgave him, and
fully restored him.

Finally, consider the storyteller: Jesus, the Son. Who better to
share the story of the Prodigal Son? This Son would soon lay down
His life as a ransom for many. This is Jesus, the Son, who at this
moment will welcome you with open arms.

Lord, help us remember the love You have for us.

God's Will for My Church

Not forsaking the assembling of ourselves together ...
—Hebrews 10:25

By becoming an active member of a local body of believers, we demonstrate our faith in God's command to participate in the body of Christ. Anything that we substitute for worship with the body of Christ (with the exception of those things that are out of necessity), becomes our god and causes us to forsake our worship. Once we become members of a local body of baptized believers, it is critical that we understand spiritual authority. The pastor of the local church provides the spiritual authority for that church and is responsible for the protection of the membership. "Obey them that have the rule over you, and submit yourselves ... as they that must give account" (Hebrews 13:17).

All Christians possess spiritual gifts that should be used for the glory of God. "But the manifestation of the Spirit is given to every man to profit withal" (1 Corinthians 12:7). We are to serve God with singleness of heart. Whatever we do, we should do it heartily, as to the Lord. As members of a local body, we should love one another, pray for one another, provide aid in sickness and distress, be slow to take offense always be ready for reconciliation, and be prepared to share the gospel.

Stewardship also requires a right attitude. We need to understand that everything belongs to the Lord. "The earth is the Lord's and the fullness thereof" (Psalm 24:1). As Christian stewards, we must properly manage two critical resources given to us from God: time and money. Time, once gone can never be replaced. We are as responsible to God for the use of our time as well as the use of our money. The tithe, often referred to as "the tenth part," was taught as an Old Testament principle. "The tenth shall be holy unto the LORD" (Leviticus 27:32).

Lord, help us to be faithful to our church as You direct.

Notes

Be Filled

Be filled with the Spirit.

—Ephesians 5:18

Like most people, our days are filled with activities, deadlines, responsibilities, commitments, and schedules for family, work, and church. Where is there time for the Holy Spirit? The entire verse reads, "And be not drunk with wine, wherein is excess; but be filled with the Spirit." Being drunk with wine merely produces a temporary sensation? Being filled with the Holy Spirit produces a permanent sensation. If we are filled with the Holy Spirit, then we should be controlled by the Holy Spirit. If we are controlled by the Spirit, we should exhibit the fruit of the Spirit: "love, joy, peace, longsuffering, gentleness, goodness, faith, meekness, temperance" (Galatians 5:22–23). The ability to exhibit the fruit of the Spirit in the life of a Christian is closely related to abiding.

> Abide in me, and I in you. As the branch cannot bear fruit of itself, except it abide in the vine … I am the vine, ye are the branches: He that abideth in me and I in him, the same bringeth forth much fruit: for without me ye can do nothing … If ye abide in me, and my words abide in you, ye shall ask what ye will, and it shall be done unto you. Herein is my Father glorified, that ye bear much fruit.
> —John 15:4–5, 7–8

Mother Teresa once said, "Our intellect and other gifts have been given to be used for God's greater glory, but sometimes they become the very god for us. … We are losing our balance when this happens. We must free ourselves to be filled by God. Even God cannot fill what is full."[6] When our activities fill our days, it is difficult for us to abide and be filled. As we abide in Christ and are filled with the Holy Spirit, we will bear much fruit.

Lord, help us to be filled with You and bear much fruit.

God's Will for My Country

Blessed is the nation whose God is the LORD.
—Psalm 33:12

Our American forefathers were men of great faith in God. On the south wall of the Lincoln Memorial, Lincoln's Gettysburg Address reads, "That these dead shall not have died in vain, that this nation under God shall have a new birth of freedom." On the north wall, Lincoln's second inaugural address reads, "It may seem strange that any men should dare to ask a just God's assistance in wringing their bread from the sweat of other men's faces. … The prayers of both could not be answered. … The Almighty has His own purposes."

From the Declaration of Independence, we read, "We hold these truths to be self-evident: that all men are created equal, that they are endowed by their Creator with certain inalienable rights." The following is from a letter George Washington received on January 4, 1786: "God who gave us life gave us liberty. Can the liberties of a nation be secure when we have removed a conviction that these liberties are the gift of God? Indeed I tremble for my country when I reflect that God is just, that his justice cannot sleep forever." Our forefathers were great men of God.

God's Word has plenty to say about the inhabitants of nations. "And I sought for a man among them that should make up the hedge, and stand in the gap before me for the land, that I should not destroy it: but I found none" (Ezekiel 22:30). "If my people … humble themselves, and pray, and seek my face, and turn from their wicked ways; then will I hear from heaven, and will forgive their sin, and will heal their land" (2 Chronicles 7:14). The Bible makes it very clear that sin will negatively affect our nation. "Righteousness exalteth a nation: but sin is a reproach to any people" (Proverbs 14:34).

Lord, help us to live righteously in our nation.

Notes

My Mother—a Virtuous Woman

Who can find a virtuous woman? For her price is far
above rubies.

—Proverbs 31:10

This passage was recorded by King Lemuel about a prophecy
taught by his mother: "Judge righteously, and plead the cause
of the poor and needy" (Proverbs 31:9). Lemuel records the
characteristics of a virtuous woman.

First, "She stretcheth out her hand to the poor ... she reacheth
forth her hands to the needy" (v. 20). My mother not only taught
this principle, but she lived it. I am reminded of the many times
when her concern and love for those less fortunate caused her to be
mindful of their needs and constantly provide assistance.

Second, "Strength and honor are her clothing" (v. 25). The most
enduring qualities about my mother were her inner strength
and unquestionable honor. From the loss of my father to battling
cancer, my mother depended on the Lord to sustain her. I attribute
this to her tremendous faith, as well as her moral and physical
courage. As honorable as anyone I have known, my mother taught
me the Lord's principle of integrity.

Third, "She openeth her mouth with wisdom; and her tongue
is the law of kindness" (v. 26). My mother seemed to always
have the right answer for all situations. She was also a master at
encouragement. She always encouraged all of her children to excel
in every endeavor.

Lastly, "Her children arise up, and call her blessed" (v. 28). I praise
the Lord for being blessed with such a wonderful, loving mother.
One day our Lord will say to her, "Well done, thou good and
faithful servant."

Lord, thank You for such a godly mother.

Notes

Prophecy Speaks

> I have spoken it, I will also bring it to pass; I have
> purposed it, I will also do it.
>
> —Isaiah 46:11

Rest assured, what God has promised, He will bring to pass. Many prophecies in God's Word have already been fulfilled. The good news is that there are other prophecies yet to be fulfilled.

Christ's birth prophesied: "Therefore the Lord himself shall give you a sign; Behold, a virgin shall conceive, and bear a son, and shall call his name Immanuel" (Isaiah 7:14).
Christ's birth fulfilled: "A virgin shall be with child...and they shall call his name Emmanuel ... Then Joseph ... took unto him his wife ... she had brought forth her firstborn son: and he called his name JESUS" (Matthew 1:23–25).

Christ's resurrection prophesied: "O LORD, thou hast brought up my soul from the grave: thou hast kept me alive, that I should not go down to the pit" (Psalm 30:3).
Christ's resurrection fulfilled: "And he saith unto them, Be not affrighted: Ye seek Jesus of Nazareth, which was crucified: he is risen; he is not here" (Mark 16:6).

Christ's return prophesied: "Our God shall come, and shall not keep silence: a fire shall devour before him, and it shall be very tempestuous round about him. He shall call to the heavens from above, and to the earth, that he may judge his people. Gather my saints together unto me; those that have made a covenant with me by sacrifice. And the heavens shall declare his righteousness: for God is judge himself. Selah" (Psalm 50:3–6). "And if I go and prepare a place for you, I will come again, and receive you unto myself" (John 14:3).
Christ's return fulfilled: Rest assured, what God has promised, He will bring to pass. Just as prophecy promised Christ's birth and resurrection, it has promised Christ's return. Are you ready?

Lord, thank You for the truth of prophecies.

Notes

Scripture References

Scripture References	1M = First Day Morning 1E = First Day Evening
Old Testament	
Genesis	
Genesis 1:11	16M
Genesis 1:16	13M
Genesis 1:26–27	16E, 25M
Genesis 1:31	16M
Genesis 2:2–3	4M
Genesis 2:9	9E, 16M
Genesis 2:16–17	16M
Genesis 2:18	19E
Genesis 2:24	7M
Genesis 3:6	9E
Genesis 3:22, 24	9E
Genesis 9:6	6M
Genesis 21:12	28M
Genesis 22:5	28M
Genesis 41:1	26M
Genesis 50:20	26M
Exodus	
Exodus 20:1	1M
Exodus 20:3	1M
Exodus 20:3-8	17M
Exodus 20:4	2M
Exodus 20:5	2M, 7M
Exodus 20:7	3M
Exodus 20:8	4M
Exodus 20:12	5M
Exodus 20:13	6M
Exodus 20:14	7M

Scripture References	1M / 1E
Exodus 20:15	8M
Exodus 20:16	9M
Exodus 20:17	10M
Exodus 31:13	4M
Exodus 31:16-17	4M
Exodus 37:7	2M
Leviticus	
Leviticus 19:11	9M
Leviticus 19:18	11M
Leviticus 27:32	29E
Numbers	
Numbers 6:24–26	18M
Deuteronomy	
Deuteronomy 5:19	8M
Deuteronomy 6:7	28E
Deuteronomy 6:9	28E
Deuteronomy 19:15	9M
Joshua	
Joshua 1:8	27E
Joshua 3:14–16	18E
Joshua 5:1	18E
Joshua 6:2	18E
Joshua 6:3	18E
Joshua 6:16	18E
Judges	
Judges 6:5–6	18M
Judges 6:16	18M
Judges 6:24	18M
1 Chronicles	
1 Chronicles 29:3	23M
1 Chronicles 29:9	23M
1 Chronicles 29:11	23M
1 Chronicles 29:14	23M
1 Chronicles 29:17	23M

2 Chronicles	
2 Chronicles 7:14	6M, 30E
Psalms	
Psalm 7:8	8M
Psalm 8:9	25E
Psalm 10:4	9E
Psalm 19:1	20M
Psalm 23:3	25E
Psalm 24:1	29E
Psalm 25:21	27E
Psalm 30:3	31E
Psalm 31:3	25E
Psalm 31:18	9M
Psalm 33:6	20M
Psalm 33:12	30E
Psalm 33:21	25E
Psalm 37:3–5	27M
Psalm 37:23	27M
Psalm 41:12	8M
Psalm 42:11	21M
Psalm 50:3–6	31E
Psalm 63:11	9M
Psalm 120:2	9M
Psalm 121:1	20E
Psalm 135:15–18	2M
Psalm 139:14	20M
Proverbs	
Proverbs 1:8	16E
Proverbs 2:3, 5	8E
Proverbs 6:10	14M
Proverbs 6:16–19	9M
Proverbs 10:18	9M
Proverbs 12:22	27E
Proverbs 14:34	30E
Proverbs 19:9	9M
Proverbs 20:7	27E

Proverbs 22:1	3M
Proverbs 22:6	28E
Proverbs 31:9	31M
Proverbs 31:10	31M
Proverbs 31:20	31M
Proverbs 31:25–26	31M
Proverbs 31:28	31M
Ecclesiastes	
Ecclesiastes 3:1	14E
Ecclesiastes 10:1	14M
Song of Solomon	
Song of Solomon 2:15	14M
Isaiah	
Isaiah 7:14	31E
Isaiah 25:8	26E
Isaiah 40:31	26M
Isaiah 44:6	2M
Isaiah 45:21	22M
Isaiah 46:11	31E
Isaiah 53:3	19M
Isaiah 53:5	19M
Isaiah 55:10–11	20E
Isaiah 58:13–14	4M
Isaiah 59:2–4	9M
Jeremiah	
Jeremiah 31:31, 33	11M
Jeremiah 31:34	13E, 20E
Jeremiah 33:3	28M
Ezekiel	
Ezekiel 22:30	30E
New Testament	
Matthew	
Matthew 1:23–25	31E
Matthew 5:14	27M
Matthew 5:16	13M, 16E
Matthew 5:23–24	13E

Matthew 5:27–28	7M		Mark 16:6	4E, 31E
Matthew 6:5	3E, 27E		**Luke**	
Matthew 6:7	15M		Luke 1:6	14E
Matthew 6:9–13	15M		Luke 1:8	14E
Matthew 6:10	7E		Luke 1:20	14E
Matthew 6:11	8M		Luke 4:8	1M
Matthew 6:14–15	13E		Luke 6:12	3E
Matthew 6:33	8E		Luke 8:17	27E
Matthew 7:7	8E		Luke 8:47	22E
Matthew 7:8	8E		Luke 9:22	19M
Matthew 7:12	14M		Luke 9:62	20E
Matthew 8:7	5E		Luke 10:40–42	15E
Matthew 9:27–30	22E		Luke 12:15	10M
Matthew 12:34	27E		Luke 13:3	22M
Matthew 16:13	21E		Luke 15:20	2E
Matthew 16:15–16	21E, 22E		Luke 15:31	29M
Matthew 18:20	19E		Luke 18:18	17M
Matthew 19:14	23E		Luke 18:20	17M
Matthew 19:20	17M		Luke 18:22–23	17M
Matthew 19:21–22	22E		Luke 23:39	1E
Matthew 21:10	21E		Luke 23:40–43	1E
Matthew 22:37–39	11M		Luke 23:41–43	12E
Matthew 22:42	21E		**John**	
Matthew 26:39	3E, 19M		John 1:3	20M
Matthew 27:22	21E		John 1:14	25M
Matthew 28:6	4E		John 3:3	12E
Matthew 28:19–20	11E		John 3:16	22M, 25M
Mark			John 4:36	19E
Mark 1:14–15	7E		John 5:30	8E
Mark 5:23	5E		John 8:12	13M
Mark 5:36–37	5E		John 10:10	15E
Mark 5:41	5E		John 10:17–18	19M
Mark 5:43	5E		John 10:27–30	25M
Mark 10:38	19M		John 11:1	15E
Mark 10:45	12E		John 11:5	15E
Mark 15:27	1E, 12E		John 11:21	12M

John 11:25	4E	1 Corinthians 5:6	14M
John 11:32–33	12M	1 Corinthians 10:13	6E
John 11:35–36	12M	1 Corinthians 11:3	28E
John 11:40	12M, 18E	1 Corinthians 12:7	11E, 29E
John 11:43	12M	1Corinthians 13:2	21M
John 11:45	12M	1 Corinthians 13:13	21M
John 12:3	15E	1 Corinthians 15:3	12E
John 13:1	11M	1 Corinthians 15:12–14	4E
John 13:33–34	11M	1 Corinthians 15:19	4E
John 14:3	31E	1 Corinthians 15:20, 22	4E
John 14:6	21E, 22M	**2 Corinthians**	
John 14:15–17	11M	2 Corinthians 4:4	13M
John 15:4–5, 7–8	30M	2 Corinthians 5:17	20E
John 15:7	8E	2 Corinthians 9:8	24E
John 16:8–11	24M	**Galatians**	
John 16:33	26E	Galatians 5:16	9E
John 19:18	1E	Galatians 5:22-23	14M, 30M
John 20:24–28	22E	**Ephesians**	
John 20:27	4E	Ephesians 2:8–9	22M
Romans		Ephesians 2:10	11E
Romans 1:17	21M	Ephesians 3:20	24E
Romans 1:20	20M	Ephesians 4:12	11E
Romans 3:11	24M	Ephesians 4:16	11E, 19E
Romans 3:23	22M	Ephesians 4:28	8M
Romans 5:12	16M	Ephesians 4:29	27E
Romans 6:23	22M	Ephesians 5:18	30M
Romans 8:17	19E	Ephesians 5:22	28E
Romans 10:9	21E, 22M	Ephesians 5:25	28E
Romans 10:13	22M	Ephesians 5:28	28E
Romans 12:5	19E	Ephesians 5:31	7M
Romans 13:9	8M	Ephesians 5:33	28E
Romans 14:12	27E	Ephesians 6:1–4	28E
Romans 15:13	21M	Ephesians 6:10	17E
1 Corinthians		Ephesians 6:12–14	17E
1 Corinthians 2:14	17M	**Philippians**	
1 Corinthians 3:9	19E	Philippians 2:13	28M

Philippians 3:21	24E		James	
Philippians 4:19	8M		James 1:5	8E
Colossians			James 1:6	5E
Colossians 1:16–17	16M		James 1:13–14	6E
Colossians 2:2	19E		James 1:13–15	10M
Colossians 2:13–15	17E		James 4:2	8E
Colossians 4:2	3E		James 4:8	27M
Colossians 3:5	10M		**1 Peter**	
1 Thessalonians			1 Peter 2:9	13M
1 Thessalonians 3:3	26E		1 Peter 2:11	9E
1 Thessalonians 4:17	19E		**2 Peter**	
1 Thessalonians 5:10	19E		2 Peter 1:3	8M
1 Thessalonians 5:17	27E		2 Peter 1:4	28M
2 Thessalonians			2 Peter 2:14	9E
2 Thessalonians 3:4	14M		**1 John**	
1 Timothy			1 John 1:5	13M
1 Timothy 2:5–6	21E, 22M		1 John 2:3–4	3E
1 Timothy 4:12	16E		1 John 2:6	3E
2 Timothy			1 John 2:10	3E
2 Timothy 1:12	22E, 24E		1 John 2:16	9E
2 Timothy 2:15	3E, 27E		1 John 3:14	14M
2 Timothy 3:16	16E		1 John 4:8	21M
Hebrews			1 John 5:12	12E
Hebrews 2:9	12E		1 John 5:13	4E
Hebrews 2:18	24E		1 John 5:14	8E
Hebrews 7:25	24E		**Jude**	
Hebrews 8:12	13E		Jude v. 24	24E
Hebrews 10:17	13E		**Revelation**	
Hebrews 10:25	19E, 29E		Revelation 3:14–16	10E
Hebrews 11:1	4E		Revelation 3:20	8E
Hebrews 11:6	6E, 8E, 21M		Revelation 14:10	19M
Hebrews 12:2	21M		Revelation 16:19	19M
Hebrews 13:5	10M, 18M, 28M			
Hebrews 13:17	29E			

Notes

1. Herschel H. Hobbs, *The Baptist Faith and Message* (Nashville, TN: Convention Press, 1971), 84.

2. Matthew Henry, *A Commentary on the Whole Bible* (Old Tappan, NJ: Fleming H. Revell Co.), 72.

3. James Strong, *The New Strong's Complete Dictionary of Bible Words* (Nashville, TN: Thomas Nelson, Inc., 1996), 24.

4. C. S. Lewis, *Mere Christianity* (New York, NY: Touchstone, Simon and Schuster Inc., 1996), 138.

5. W. E. Vine, *Expository of New Testament Words* (Peabody, MA: Hendrickson Publishers, 1989), 411.

6. E. Draper, *Draper's Book of Quotations for the Christian World* (Wheaton: Tyndale House, 1992), 109.

CPSIA information can be obtained
at www.ICGtesting.com
Printed in the USA
FSHW010741300619
59582FS